Praise for
THE GUARDIAN GATEWAY

"Kim Wilborn has crafted a well-written, easy-to-use guide that introduces you to the Guardians that you can consciously connect with, ones that can provide guidance and inspiration on our soul's journey. She offers solid advice on how you can transform your life and move forward in a new way with the help of these Guardians."

— **Dr. Steven Farmer**, author, psychotherapist, and shamanic practitioner

"I count myself fortunate to know Kim and have co-created much Magic with her and the nature spirits through the Guardian Gateway *Telesummits. I really enjoyed reading* The Guardian Gateway, *which provides a very grounded yet loving portal into accessing the wisdom of the ethereal and celestial kingdoms. Read this beautiful guide with an open heart and a pen and paper at hand, as you'll want to enjoy the many explorative journeys along the way!"*

— **Calista**, award-winning author of *Unicorn Rising* and *The Female Archangels*, founder of Unicorn Healing® and Angel Healing®

"Empowering and beautifully written with practical advice, meditations, and visualizations to support you on your spiritual path. Kim's knowledge and loving desire to assist us all in achieving our highest and best in life radiates through each page. The Guardian Gateway *welcomes you to a world of support from the hidden realms— beings who are bursting to share their knowledge and support with us if we just open up to listen and acknowledge them.*

"Delightfully uplifting, this book will inspire you to deepen your connection with your Guardians to be the person you came to Earth to be—your true authentic self of radiant light! Enjoy!"

— **Alphedia Arara**, author of *Messages from Nature's Guardians* and *Ascending with Unicorns*, founder of the Dragon Wisdom School

THE
GUARDIAN
GATEWAY

Hay House Titles of Related Interest

YOU CAN HEAL YOUR LIFE, *the movie,* **starring Louise Hay & Friends**
(available as a 1-DVD program, an expanded 2-DVD set,
and an online streaming video)
Learn more at www.hayhouse.com/louise-movie

THE SHIFT, the movie,
starring Dr. Wayne W. Dyer
(available as a 1-DVD program, an expanded 2-DVD set,
and an online streaming video)
Learn more at www.hayhouse.com/the-shift-movie

❧

*Angel Numbers: The Message and Meaning Behind 11:11
and Other Number Sequences* by Kyle Gray

*Animal Spirit Guides: An Easy-to-Use Handbook for Identifying and Understanding
Your Power Animals and Animal Spirit Helpers* by Steven D. Farmer, Ph.D.

*Ask Your Guides: Calling in Your Divine Support System for Help
with Everything in Life* by Sonia Choquette

Dragons: Your Celestial Guardians by Diana Cooper

*The Seven Types of Spirit Guide: How to Connect and Communicate
with Your Cosmic Helpers* by Yamile Yemoonyah

Unicorn Rising: Live Your Truth and Unleash Your Magic by Calista

❧

All of the above are available at your local bookstore,
or may be ordered by visiting:

Hay House USA: www.hayhouse.com®
Hay House Australia: www.hayhouse.com.au
Hay House UK: www.hayhouse.co.uk
Hay House India: www.hayhouse.co.in

THE
GUARDIAN
GATEWAY

Working with
Unicorns, Dragons, Angels, Tree Spirits,
and Other Spiritual Guardians

KIM WILBORN

HAY HOUSE, INC.
Carlsbad, California • New York City
London • Sydney • New Delhi

Copyright © 2021 by Kim Wilborn

Published in the United States by: Hay House, Inc.: www.hayhouse.com®
Published in Australia by: Hay House Australia Pty. Ltd.: www.hayhouse.com.au
Published in the United Kingdom by: Hay House UK, Ltd.: www.hayhouse.co.uk
Published in India by: Hay House Publishers India: www.hayhouse.co.in

Cover design: Kathleen Lynch • *Interior design:* Nick C. Welch

All rights reserved. No part of this book may be reproduced by any mechanical, photographic, or electronic process, or in the form of a phonographic recording; nor may it be stored in a retrieval system, transmitted, or otherwise be copied for public or private use—other than for "fair use" as brief quotations embodied in articles and reviews—without prior written permission of the publisher.

The author of this book does not dispense medical advice or prescribe the use of any technique as a form of treatment for physical, emotional, or medical problems without the advice of a physician, either directly or indirectly. The intent of the author is only to offer information of a general nature to help you in your quest for emotional, physical, and spiritual well-being. In the event you use any of the information in this book for yourself, the author and the publisher assume no responsibility for your actions.

**Cataloging-in-Publication Data is on file
with the Library of Congress**

Tradepaper ISBN: 978-1-4019-6128-2
E-book ISBN: 978-1-4019-6129-9

10 9 8 7 6 5 4 3 2 1
1st edition, July 2021

Printed in the United States of America

To the Guardians and all who love them

CONTENTS

PREFACE

One day several years ago, I heard someone on a telesummit talking about "Unicorn Healing." My first response was to roll my eyes, but I couldn't—because I was getting a strong sense from my inner guidance that Unicorns are real. Surprised, I tuned in to my guidance and asked, "Well, if Unicorns actually exist, what other mythological beings are real?"

The answer came back right away: *Dragons.*

I went into the nearest bathroom to be alone and closed my eyes. Into my mind came the image of my Guardian Dragon standing in front of me. I could feel its energetic presence.

In that moment, my life expanded. As I opened myself up to the possibility of other spiritual Guardians, I began to connect with an ever-growing team of Guardian Beings—Unicorns, Dragons, and Angels at first, then Trees, the Earth Soul, and more.

I already knew that each one of us incarnates with a unique soul purpose. Now I came to understand that each one of us also incarnates with our own team of spiritual Guardians. These beings are dedicated to helping us create a life that *fully* expresses that soul purpose.

Regularly connecting with my Guardians transformed every part of my life, and eventually I began hosting my own telesummits, all focused on helping people connect with Guardian Beings. I saw how eager people are to connect with Guardian Beings, and I began to see how much these Guardians can help each one of us express our gifts and fulfill our own soul purpose. I created a website called the Guardian Gateway and devoted myself to creating sacred spaces—energetic gateways—in which people could meet and partner with their spiritual Guardians.

MY OWN TALE OF DOWNS AND UPS

I *know* you want to create a life of purpose and love, a life that fits who you truly are on a deep level. And I know you've had challenges that have kept you from that goal. You might be needing a way to recenter yourself and get back to your place of power, even with all the worry and anxiety in the world, because you know you have gifts within you that you haven't fully expressed yet.

You may feel a burning desire to bring positive energy into the world every day, even if you're not sure how. You might even feel you're meant to live more than an ordinary life—that your life is meant to be bigger, with greater meaning.

I understand all of these feelings because I felt this way for *years*.

My spiritual awakening came in the form of a daytime talk show. Spiritual author Marianne Williamson was the guest, and as she spoke, I found myself uplifted in a way I'd never felt before. Soon I was reading the book she mentioned, *A Course in Miracles*, and attending local classes on it. As I studied the book (a nondenominational text designed to bring about spiritual transformation), I felt as if a giant, invisible doorway was opening within me. I found that I loved to discuss the *Course* with others, so I decided to teach my own weekly classes.

I would start each class by reading a passage from the *Course* and opening a discussion. Inevitably, the people in the class would bring up their personal problems and challenges, and as they did, I found I was receiving guidance that could help them transform their problems and grow into their fullest selves.

Along with the guidance I was receiving about their current issues, I also had a sudden "knowing" about the issue at the *core* of their current problems. People in the classes began asking me to counsel them, and so for many years I had a transformational counseling practice helping individuals, couples, and even business owners. In the evenings I held women's circles and workshops, all aimed at helping people reconnect with their true selves and live from their soul purpose. I had no special training or certification (although I did get a hypnosis certification along the way). I just relied on the inner knowing that came into my awareness as a client spoke.

In the beginning I was a bit afraid to relay this inner knowing to my clients, but every time I did, my clients confirmed that it was true. For instance, a client might be telling me about a problem she was having with her boyfriend, and suddenly an idea of something totally unrelated would come to me.

"Does the way you feel have something to do with your sister?" I'd ask. An expression of knowing would come into the client's eyes, and she would confirm the truth of what I'd said. Guidance would then come to me about how to transform her problem.

Years of experiencing that "knowing" and having it confirmed has left me trusting it completely. I watched as my clients got more and more into alignment with their authentic selves, and started living out the soul purpose they had come into the world to express.

As the years went on, my spiritual path led me on from *A Course in Miracles* to studies of the Goddess and the Law of Attraction as I became more and more in touch with my own inner guidance. I felt that my work was an expression of my soul purpose, and the feeling I had when I was teaching or counseling was transcendent.

Just as my work success was at an all-time high, my marriage started to break up. In the wake of the emotional roller coaster, my personal vibration was at an all-time low.

I pulled away from my counseling practice to work on healing myself, which—although necessary—had a terrible effect on my finances. My divorce coincided with the recession that began in the United States in 2008, and I ended up going bankrupt, losing my house, and moving in with my elderly parents. *Gulp.*

I'd lost the health benefits I'd had when I was married, so I got a job working at Starbucks for 20 hours a week, which was the minimum you had to work to qualify for the company's health plan. I felt like I had a capital *L* for Loser tattooed on my forehead. But I knew I couldn't give up on my work. It was my North Star, the thing that gave my life meaning. It was the thing that kept me going when everything was at its darkest.

I knew I had a mission to fulfill, and I knew it involved helping large numbers of people.

When I'd worked in my office seeing counseling clients, I'd always wished that my work could reach more people and that I could have a positive impact on a greater number of people's lives.

Now, living at my parents' house, I broadcast weekly online radio shows and worked at creating an online counseling practice. But no matter what I did or how hard I tried, I just couldn't seem to attract a large audience.

In order to deal with my less-than-desirable current life, I surrounded myself with spiritual wisdom, soaking up the goodness of every free webinar or telesummit I could find. It was on one such telesummit that I was first made aware of Unicorns as living beings.

ENTER THE GUARDIANS

With the revelation of the existence of the Guardian Beings, it was as if, having endured a long, long winter, spring was now here. As I spent regular time connecting with my Guardian team, my life began to change. New insights, new ideas, and new opportunities started coming into my life.

Six months later, I was taking notes on the final day at a live business-building event when the speaker casually mentioned that holding telesummits was a good way to build a bigger audience. I felt a jolt of electricity go through my body as I realized that this was what I *had* to do next.

A telesummit is an online event consisting of multi-speaker interviews, which listeners can access from anywhere in the world. I had absolutely no idea of how to put one together—in fact, the very idea was terrifying! But my inner drive kept propelling me forward, and as I communed with my Guardian team of Dragons, Unicorns, and Angels, my first (small) telesummit became a reality.

The telesummit wasn't a financial success, but I didn't care. It was a huge achievement for me, and I felt so empowered! I decided to create another event devoted to Guardian Beings as my way of giving thanks for all the ways they were supporting me.

This event was my breakthrough. Listeners loved the telesummit calls, and lots of them let me know that learning about Guardian

Beings was changing their lives. And this time, the event was a financial success.

I immediately quit my job at Starbucks and devoted myself to creating telesummits and online programs on the subjects I loved: the Goddess, the Guardian Spirits of Nature, Faery Allies, Crystal and Stone Guardians, Spirit Animals, Tree Spirits, the Sacred Earth, Guardian Ancestors, the Spiritual Path of Tarot, the Guardian Planets of Astrology, and more. Each event focused on the Guardian aspect of the theme. I learned—and continue to learn—so much from the wide variety of teachers I interview.

I'd found my sweet spot—making a living from doing the work I loved *and* helping large numbers of people. I moved out of my parents' home and into a house on my favorite river, with a boat dock in my backyard. (This is heaven for me, because it allows me to connect with the Spirit of Water every day!)

My work with Guardian Beings continues to expand in wondrous ways, and I'm so excited to welcome you into this sacred space with me so you can experience your own story of expansion and wonder!

INTRODUCTION

Many of us love the *idea* of Unicorns or Dragons, but we're blocked by the belief that they aren't physical beings. We tend to think about these beings in a fanciful way, without making them an actual part of our lives—without having a daily, *personal* relationship with them.

That's where I come in. I'm here to help you learn how to work with Guardian Beings in *practical* ways that will make a real difference in your life. We are always in the presence of Guardian Beings. But unless we're consciously engaging with them, we don't always feel their presence.

In this book I'll help you connect to Guardian Beings and bring them into your daily reality. Then, partnering with your Guardian team, you'll gain new skills that will help you move past challenges that have kept you from fulfilling your own beautiful potential.

Guardian Beings come in many different forms, but they're all here to help us—and all the beings of the Earth—evolve and expand into our full, radiant potentials. They do this by uplifting us with the energy of love, bringing solutions to our everyday problems, and assisting us in everything we do. Our Guardians help us discover and live our soul purpose, raise our vibration (thus improving what we attract into our experience), manifest our heart-based desires, and gain the wisdom and support we need to live our best life.

There are many, many Guardian Beings supporting us. We'll focus on five in this book: Dragons, Unicorns, Angels, Trees, and the Earth Soul (Spirit of the Earth). You'll learn how to create a deep connection with each one, and you'll also learn how to connect with various other Guardians throughout the chapters. Your relationship with them will be unique because it will be based upon *your* unique soul purpose.

I don't personally see Guardian Beings, but I sense their presence through my heart—and you can, too. If you close your eyes and see a Guardian taking shape in your imagination, know that the form you perceive is not as important as the energy you feel. Through this book, you'll form relationships that will give you firsthand knowledge about Guardian Beings. I'd love for you to share what you learn at www.KimWilborn.com and add to an ever-growing body of knowledge about spiritual Guardians.

DISCOVER YOUR DIVINE BLUEPRINT AND YOUR GREATER SELF

At first glance, this book might seem to be about Guardian Beings. But this book is really about *you* and your personal journey to fulfill your divine blueprint.

Each of us comes into life with a unique soul purpose—our own original blueprint—and we also come into life with a team of Guardian Beings to help us create a life that matches that blueprint. It's important to note that there's no be-all-and-end-all purpose for us to discover. Our sacred purpose can take many forms, and it's something that unfolds for each of us over time—finding new ways to express itself every day.

You may have a good sense of the essence of your soul purpose, or you may feel unsure. Either way, here's something to keep in mind: when you are truly engaged with and expressing your purpose, you're spending the majority of your time engaged in activities that *enliven* you. It's the opposite of the feeling we experience when we feel stuck.

I used to think of the things that habitually kept me stuck as *blocks*, and I tailored my programs to help people move past whatever was blocking them from expressing their soul purpose. But with time, I've realized that it's less a matter of having blocks, and more a matter of lacking *skills*. This was a liberating discovery, because *skills are something each one of us can gain!*

I can't stress this enough: with guidance, practice, and the support of your Guardians, you can gain all the skills you need in order to express your soul purpose in a magical, life-expanding way.

In the pages that follow, you'll get in touch with your original divine blueprint and learn how Guardian Beings can help you align with that blueprint to *fully* express your soul purpose. The more you consciously connect with the Guardians, the easier it is to create in alignment with your Greater Self, bringing the energy of what you love into physical form. The Greater Self is what I call the eternal part of you that exists throughout all your lifetimes, the part that's completely in alignment with your spiritual truth and power.

Every person has a Greater Self. We also have the mundane "everyday self" that forms our identity as we go through life. When you experience ongoing problems it's because, in that particular place in your life, your identity is out of alignment with your Greater Self and the sacred purpose you're meant to express.

When you create a daily, conscious relationship with your personal Guardian team, you can call forth as much help as you need, whenever you need it. Their help may come in the form of inspiration, new ideas, new solutions, and new manifestations. As you go through life, you can partner with more and more Guardian Beings, becoming part of a larger team of beings all working on behalf of love and expansion.

Resist the tendency to place Guardian Beings on a pedestal while thinking of yourself as a lesser being. As a human, you are a valuable partner and a vital member of the team. In fact, living in awareness of yourself as a being who is part of a vast group of beings working together to expand and uplift life is, itself, a spiritual path.

If you think of Guardian Beings the way you think of people, it will be hard to imagine how they can be in so many places at so many different times or how they would want to be bothered with trivial requests or things that don't seem important or worthy. But if you see Guardians for what they are—loving, supportive energies who are here to help you create every part of the life you're meant to live—it changes everything. This allows you to connect with them in a way that sustains you *both*.

YOUR HEART IS A GATEWAY

A Gateway is a meeting place, an energetic bridge between dimensions. Sometimes it's an energetic place to meet with high-vibration nonphysical beings or energies, and sometimes it's an energetic space within which you gain an expanded awareness of a physical Guardian—for example, connecting to a Tree as a conscious being.

These Gateways form stable energetic spaces through which we connect. More than open doorways, they are *sacred spaces* that hold us as we commune with Guardian Beings.

Guardian Gateways are created out of love—a Gateway springs into being whenever someone opens her (or his) heart to connect with a Guardian. We tend these Guardian Gateways by *consistently* connecting through our hearts to the Guardians that meet us there.

To create these energetic spaces, we use the sacred power of our imagination. Some believe the imagination is only good for "pretending," but in fact your imagination is the mechanism by which you create your life experiences. Your imagination designs the inner structures that your creative energy pours into, and that in turn determines the outer structures you experience in your life.

You can use this mechanism (your imagination) right now to create an interdimensional bridge between your physical reality and your own team of Guardian Beings.

Create a Guardian Gateway Now

Take a slow, deep breath. Now let it out and go within yourself. Feel yourself grounded into the Earth's embrace with energetic roots connecting you to the Earth's love. . . . Now go even deeper within.

Keep breathing slowly as you go deeper and deeper, until you begin to see a beautiful building, sparkling with magical energy. Your name is engraved in large letters over the wide front doors.

Feel yourself entering through these doors to stand in a huge, beautiful room filled with golden light. Soak in the sense of warmth, safety, and belonging that fills this room. Take a moment to feel this special place being absorbed into your heart, where it will be kept safe and pure.

Take another deep breath and come back into your physical surroundings. Ground yourself into the Earth's embrace once more.

You've just created the beginnings of the interdimensional bridge that you'll use throughout this book.

HOW TO USE THIS BOOK

The Guardian Gateway is an invitation to a sacred group space for you and all who read it. Knowing that we are all together in this space is a powerful part of the experience. That's why I use the words *us* and *our* as well as *you* throughout the book.

I've capitalized the words that represent Guardian Beings and the divine in general. I hope that each time you see the word *Tree* with a capital *T* (for example), you'll be once again reminded that Trees are powerful Guardian Beings and not just part of the scenery!

In Part I of this book, you'll learn how to work with five Guardian Beings—Dragons, Unicorns, Angels, Tree Spirits, and the Earth Soul—who are here to support you in every way. The chapters begin and end with an invocation. Say them to yourself, silently or aloud, and really *feel* the words. At the end of the chapter, notice the deeper meaning given to the invocation by your connection with the Guardian.

Part II will help you create a powerful new foundation starting with the all-important skill of self-love, which you'll access in a totally new way. Then you'll learn how to open to new possibilities, give yourself permission, trust yourself, reinvent yourself, open to receive, find your true voice, make peace with where you are, upgrade your self-talk, and release the past—all with the help of Guardian Beings.

In Part III you'll learn how to be yourself, free yourself from worrying about what other people think, forgive in a new way, tell yourself a new story, reclaim your spark, focus on what you *want*, claim and enforce your boundaries, become a caretaker of consciousness, support yourself with love, expect the best, dream bigger, and finally move forward into an expanded life, connected to the sacred energetic space we share.

In addition to Unicorns, Dragons, Angels, Tree Spirits, and the Earth Soul, you'll be introduced to other living Guardian energies throughout this book. Some chapters will focus on mindset shifts, some are filled with exercises and journeys to guide you through your own inner changes, and others are a mix of both. Do the exercises in your head; write them down in a journal; or, for a richer, guided experience, you can get my *Guardian Gateway Activation Experience*, which contains 29 videos and more than 60 illustrated transformation sheets. (For more information, please go to www.KimWilborn.com/activation-experience.)

The best way to experience the transformation of *The Guardian Gateway* is to read the whole book through, in order. Then if you like, you can spend a week or even a month with each one of the Guardian chapters. Return to the chapters in Parts II and III as needed or reread them in order, spending a week or more focusing on each skill in depth.

Important Note: Sometimes when I'm reading a book, I skip over the exercises I come across, so I can stay in the flow of the story. I think to myself, *I'll just read that exercise when I have time to do it* or *I'll just read all the exercises together at the end of the book.* Please don't do that with this book!

The exercises and journeys (which are set off in a special italicized font) are an integral part of this story, and without them, you won't be able to have the direct experiences that will connect you to the Guardian energies that will in turn transform your life. Please read each exercise as you come to it, even if you can't fully go within and do the exercise right away. Just reading them will allow them to begin working magic in your life. For a deeper experience, go back when you can and spend more time with each journey.

After each guided journey or exercise is complete, take a few moments to come fully back into your body. Always remember to say thank you (even if I don't remind you)! Saying thank you will remind you that you're not engaged in mental exercises—instead, you're connecting with real living, loving beings.

I will ask you to ground yourself many, many times in this book. By this I mean dropping energetic roots and grounding deeply into the energy and love of the Earth. Connect to the energy of your own heart, then imagine that energy flowing down through your body and into the Earth, creating a powerful "root system." Feel the Earth embrace your energetic roots and send loving, nurturing energy back up into your body. This will bring you out of being "too much in your head," and into a state of sacred balance between spirit and form.

ONE MORE THING, BEFORE YOU START

I'll be sharing my experiences in this book based on my own perceptions, but yours may be different, so I support you in developing your *own* understanding of Guardian Beings. Run everything I say through the filter of your own inner knowing, and take away only the ideas that feel true to *you*. Trust your own intuition in all things!

I believe the purpose of life on Earth is to bring the energy of love into physical form. As we journey through this book together, it's my hope that you'll begin to see more and more of the things you love take shape around you and that you'll create lasting relationships with Guardian Beings that will transform your life—and our world.

I believe there are many of us who incarnated at this time to work with Guardians and each other, and I'm devoted to everyone in this group—both Guardian Beings and humans. Together we create energetic space in which we can fulfill our full potential and share *all* our gifts with the world.

This may take the form of being a teacher or healer, but not necessarily! You can share your gifts simply by showing up authentically in your life, fully expressing who you are and what you love.

Your relationships with the Guardians are also a gift you share with the world. By connecting with Guardian Beings on a regular basis, you become a Gateway Guardian, bringing the sacred energy of the Guardians with you wherever you go.

My wish for you is that you recognize and live more and more as who you truly are, feeling a greater sense of "rightness" within yourself every day—supported, surrounded, and loved by the Guardian Beings who are here to help you express *all* the beauty within you.

Once you have developed deep, ongoing relationships with your Guardian team and have gained the skills that will help you show up in life "all the way," you will reach a new level of being. That will be the starting point for a whole new chapter of life—one that you can't even imagine now.

I am excited for you, and excited for the world as it prepares itself to receive your gifts!

> Go to KimWilborn.com/Bonus to get your free Guardian Gateway Expansion Bonus. This bonus includes special telesummit call recordings to help you create relationships with each Guardian plus an extra skill, Create a Personal Mission Statement, which will give you additional support as you journey through the book.

PART I

MEET YOUR GUARDIANS

You can use all the exercises and journeys as is, in the way that works best for you. But if you find you want more help going deeply within, use the following guided journey as a preamble to the journeys you take in this book. (You'll find a copy of this journey in the Appendix for easy access.)

Take a deep breath; let it out slowly as you prepare to fully enter the sacred space we are creating together. With each breath, feel yourself relaxing more and more.

Allow yourself to feel a beautiful beam of Source energy entering through the top of your head. Let this energy flow down into your body, into every part of your being. Feel it filling your entire body, flowing through your feet, and beaming down into the center of the Earth.

At the center of the Earth, feel the presence of a huge glowing crystal, filled with positive energy and love for you. See the beam of

1

Source energy flow down into the crystal, harmonize with the energy there, and beam straight back up into you.

Feel this beautiful energy flow up through the soles of your feet, into your knees, up into your hips, your chest, your arms, your throat, and your head. Feel it filling your heart and spreading out all around you . . . and now feel it spread out to encompass the whole world. See the whole planet held in a space of safety and love.

Within this space of love and safety, feel yourself become centered.

Feel yourself become grounded.

Feel yourself become balanced.

And feel yourself become whole.

Now come back to your own heart, and from that heart space, open to connect with high-vibration Guardian Beings in all their many forms. Feel the beautiful, pure life force within you.

Feel the loving life force of the Earth supporting you, and feel the wisdom and love in the Guardian Energies all around you.

Feel yourself a vital part of this whole, and take your place in the creative tapestry of life that we are all weaving . . . together.

Now come back to your normal waking state, and send your energetic roots deeply down into the loving Earth.

Feel yourself fully in your body, and wiggle your fingers and toes for a few moments. Look around at the room or space you are in, and feel every part of your body full of the energy of life and love.

CHAPTER 1

❧

MEET YOUR DRAGON GUARDIANS

Dragon Invocation

*We call upon the Dragons
to partner with us
in creation.
May we know you
and love you,
and may we
always be uplifted
by the strength
of your wings.*

Each of us has access to a Guardian Dragon. We need only open our hearts, connect, and consistently invest our energy in order to create a lasting, ongoing relationship.

When I first began opening myself to connect with Dragons, I was surprised at how much they are about love: the courage to love, the power to love, and the willingness to open your heart. Dragons also hold the energies of wisdom, awakening, empowerment, and creation. They are powerful Guardians and friends, helping us to know ourselves, live and love from our true power, and awaken to new levels of being.

When we think of Dragons, we often think of protection, and it's true that Dragons bring with them a powerful sense of safety. But focusing on a need for protection is disempowering and can keep us stuck in a place of fear. So instead of asking for protection, I like to call forth the energy of safety. When you call on the Dragons to help you feel safe, they bring with them not only safety, but a powerful love as well.

For instance, I used to have a cool (but unreliable) classic car. One day, on a long drive home from the beach, I started to worry about whether the car would make it all the way back. I called on the Dragons, expecting to feel them flying overhead. Instead, I felt a powerful, loving female Dragon presence immediately behind me. Her wings wrapped around me and filled me with so much love and support that I forgot to worry about the car, and I had a magical ride home.

As you get to know the Dragons, focus on what you would love to create in your life. Call on them when you need to feel safe and when you need help reconnecting to your own true power, but don't *only* call on them at those times. Partner with your Guardian Dragon to bring forth all the beauty and love within you.

MEET YOUR GUARDIAN DRAGON

Having your own experience is more valuable than any amount of learning from others, so let's create a Gateway for you to meet your own Dragon Guardian.

Connect with the energy of your own heart, and from that heart space, open to connect with all the high-vibrational Guardian Beings who are here to help you, who love you and want only the best for you.

Set an intention to align yourself with your highest good, and ask to meet your Guardian Dragon. Feel yourself grounded into the Earth's embrace, and go even deeper within.

Go deeper and deeper, until you come to a place where you see the same beautiful building from our introduction, still sparkling with magical energy. See your name engraved in large letters over the wide front doors.

Feel yourself entering this building now to stand in the beautiful room filled with golden light. Let the sense of warmth, safety, and belonging that fills this room fill you as well.

As the light fills your being, you begin to see a wide door before you, and you open it and step out into a beautiful meadow. Here you feel the morning sun warming your face and a fresh breeze on your skin.

You look up and see a small dot in the bright-blue sky. As you watch, this dot becomes larger and larger, until you see it is a beautiful Dragon flying toward you.

As the Dragon approaches, the air around you changes, becoming charged with joyful energy. It's almost as if you can see sparkling colors dancing in the air, and you feel your own heart responding with a feeling of pure happiness.

Now your Guardian Dragon lands on the grass before you and looks deeply into your eyes. Stay grounded to the Earth and centered in your heart as you connect to its presence.

Commune with this Dragon for as long as you like, absorbing the love, wisdom, and support it has for you.

When you are ready, thank your Guardian Dragon for its presence. As you watch, the Dragon fades to invisibility, but you can still feel its presence and the powerful guiding energy it radiates.

Now close your inner eyes, and when you open them, you are back in your physical surroundings.

Feel yourself fully in your body, move your arms and legs, and take a nice deep breath.

Ground yourself once more into the love of the Earth and return to your normal waking state, feeling the presence of your Guardian Dragon at your side.

Once you have connected with a Dragon Guardian, you may find yourself going on a spontaneous journey *within* the journey above. It may feel like a movie is unfolding within your mind's eye. When I experience this, I consciously take part in whatever story is unfolding, knowing that through this inner journey either the Dragon is helping me in my evolution, or I am helping the Dragon in its work.

A few years ago I was invited to the annual Fairy Congress in Washington State to teach about Dragon Guardians. My class was held in a beautiful meadow, exactly like the one in our guided journey (even though I'd written the journey years before).

It was an amazing feeling to stand in this real-life meadow and lead a group through the guided journey. I could feel the presence of Dragons all around, swooping down to connect with the people around me.

The participants were so moved by the Dragon connections they made that day, and I was so grateful, as always, to the Dragons!

DISCOVERING YOUR SHARED INTENTION

Discovering an intention that you and your Guardian Dragon share is a powerful way to deepen your relationship. This is something you can choose to do one time for an overarching intention or on a daily basis to connect with a shared purpose for each new day.

Take a deep breath, let it out slowly, and ground yourself down into the Earth's embrace. Spend a few moments feeling the presence of your Guardian Dragon before you.

Open your heart, and ask your Guardian Dragon for a single word. Once you get a sense of this word, write it down.

Place this word where you will see it often. (And if you don't get a sense of the word right away, don't worry. Keep your heart open to receive it in the days to come.)

You can also use this process to connect to the Dragons when you need their wisdom and guidance. Recently I tuned in to my Guardian Dragon, opened my heart, and asked for a single word. Immediately my busy mind started producing words like *wisdom* and *knowledge*. Then I felt the word *open* powerfully enter my consciousness, carrying with it the energy of the Dragons.

I realized that, without knowing it, I'd been stuck in a kind of uptight, focused-on-getting-things-done mode. I gratefully relaxed into the energy of openness, feeling the loving Dragon energy all around me.

DRAGONS AND EMPOWERMENT

One of the things Dragons do is help us become emotionally empowered. To me, being emotionally empowered means that I love myself and that I believe I deserve to have the things I want.

It's a big deal!

Thinking about getting what we want can be scary, not only because we're afraid we don't deserve it, but also because we're afraid we might not like it once we get it.

I believe the true desires of your heart come from your Greater Self and your divine blueprint, and when you partner with the Dragons in creating your life, you can count on their wisdom to help bring things into form that will align with your highest good and serve your life at the highest level.

Take a moment now and say these words to yourself: emotionally empowered. *What do you feel in your body as you continue to repeat these words? Do you notice any sensations, and if so, where in your body do you feel them?*

Continue repeating, then check in again. Do you notice any new sensations?

Keep the idea of being emotionally empowered in your awareness as we move forward together.

DEEPENING THE RELATIONSHIP

Continue to deepen your relationship by bringing your Guardian Dragon into your awareness throughout the day.

Take a deep breath and ground yourself in the love of the Earth.
Invite your Guardian Dragon to stand in front of you.

What do you sense?

How does it feel?

Open your heart now and feel the love this Guardian has for you.
Take this love with you as you walk in the world.

Over time, as you consciously connect and open your heart, you'll be able to feel the presence of your Dragon Guardian more and more powerfully—and the effects of this connection will be powerfully felt in your life and in the world.

We'll close this chapter with the words of our Dragon invocation, made more meaningful now by the connection you've made with your own Guardian Dragon.

We call upon the Dragons
to partner with us
in creation.
May we love you
and trust you,
and may we
always be uplifted
by the strength
of your wings.

CHAPTER 2

MEET YOUR UNICORN GUARDIANS

Unicorn Invocation

We call now to the Unicorns.
Come into our awareness
so that we may know you
and work alongside you
as you joyfully uplift
the energy of this world.
Be our Guardians and companions
as we journey through life, and please
repair,
upgrade,
and maintain
our personal energy fields,
so that we may live
as our best,
most radiant,
and most powerfully beautiful selves.

I used to think of Unicorns as imaginary fantasy creatures, but I've come to know they are actually real beings vibrating at a very high frequency. Throughout time we've connected with them in our visions and dreams, which is why we've always drawn pictures of them and told stories about them.

When you consciously create a relationship with Unicorn Guardians, you anchor their energy into our physical reality, which raises the vibration of this reality, allowing it to improve and evolve. In other words, you can support them in their work *simply by knowing they are here.*

When I first became intuitively aware of the Unicorns as actual beings, I tried to tune in to what they are here for and how they work. I got a strong sense of the Unicorns working to repair, maintain, and upgrade the Earth's energy grid.

An image came to my mind of the Unicorns circling the Earth like a maypole, weaving strands of energy and creating patterns in the world's energy grid to help us upgrade our lives and evolve. (They do this for our personal energy systems as well.)

CONNECTING WITH THE UNICORNS FOR MAGICAL CHANGE

Unicorns purify our energy and clear whatever's blocking us from living our original divine blueprint. They light up the path before us and help us make a clear space in which to create a new future.

Connect to the energy in your own heart, and open yourself to accept the love and help of your personal Guardian team.

Set an intention to align yourself with your highest good, and ask now to meet your Guardian Unicorn. Feel yourself grounded into the Earth's embrace, and go even deeper within.

Go deeper and deeper, until you find yourself in a beautiful moonlit forest clearing. The air smells sweet, and you feel safe and loved. Into the clearing come several Unicorns, beautiful and shining white. Feel the air sparkle as the energy around you begins to dance.

Feel the Unicorns purifying your energy as you gaze at them, one by one. Feel them clearing your path and raising your vibration— giving you a new, higher vibration template.

Feel the love they have for you, and allow your heart to be lifted to a new level. Know that these Unicorn Beings are here for you—and for the world—to release the pain of the past, wash away old negativity, and upgrade your energetic field.

They are here to bring us into a new light-filled era.

Embrace each Unicorn and give it your love. Then, open to receive a gift in return.

Open your hands and look down to see the gift they've given you. Hold it in your heart and feel it find its home there.

Now watch the Unicorns fade to invisibility, even though you know they are still there. Know you can connect with them anytime you like. You can also invite them to be anyplace in the world that needs their energy.

Now breathe deeply as you come back to your normal waking state, moving your arms and legs, and feeling yourself in your body.

Return to the physical world with the beauty and magic of the Unicorns filling you and shining all around you.

UNICORN HEALING

When I first started connecting with Unicorns, I focused my attention on their horns.

One day I asked the Unicorns for a healing and immediately got the sense of a beautiful Unicorn standing in front of me, pointing healing energy from its horn to a space above my head.

It was soon joined by three more Unicorns—one on either side and one behind me—all focusing healing energy to the same spot above my head.

I tried to imagine the healing beams moving lower to point at my head, but the Unicorns remained exactly as they were for several minutes.

I remembered later that the eighth chakra is located above the head, and I realized that the Unicorns knew *exactly* where I needed their healing energy most.

Take a deep breath, ground yourself into the Earth, and invite into your presence your Guardian Unicorn. Imagine it standing in front of you, gazing down into your eyes.

Feel the energy from its horn filling you with cleansing, clearing, and uplifting energy.

Now imagine yourself as a Unicorn, with powerful energy beaming out from your brow chakra. Feel the beauty and grace inherent in all Unicorns, and feel yourself at one with this grace now.

When I ask for help from the Unicorns, sometimes more than one appears, and nowadays I often feel two Guardian Unicorns that stand at my sides.

Recently I was headed into the grocery store feeling incredibly grouchy at the thought of all the shopping ahead of me. I asked the Unicorns for help, and connected with the presence of my Guardian Unicorns at my sides.

Into my mind came the image of a rainbow stretching over my head, with each end coming down into the Unicorns. So corny, right? But all at once, I felt better! I believe we associate Unicorns with rainbows for a reason.

HELPING UNICORNS IN THEIR WORK

As time goes on, you may feel called to help the Unicorns in their work. I do this through inner journeying, connecting to the Unicorns as we've done here, then (as I mentioned in the previous chapter) allowing a scene to unfold in my mind's eye.

I've most often experienced inner journeys in which I'm opening portals and helping to create connections between realms. (This may be because creating Gateways is part of my soul purpose; your work with them might involve something completely different!)

Remember, you are not a lesser being in relation to the Unicorns. You are a vital part of a sacred team, and human beings have roles to play in the evolution of our world that can only be accomplished by us!

Relax and have an open mind as you journey with the Unicorns, allowing your own intuition to guide you.

MORNING UNICORN MEDITATION

You can create your own daily Unicorns practice with a Morning Unicorn Meditation.

Drop energetic roots down into the loving Earth, and feel Source energy flowing into your heart. Feel this Source love creating a space of safety, and feel it spread out all around you, until it encompasses the whole world.

See the whole planet held in this space of safety. Now come back to your own heart. From that heart space, allow yourself to go deeper within until you find yourself in a place filled with light. Your body feels light and buoyant, grounded and centered—all at the same time.

You become aware of a beautiful Unicorn standing at your side. You reach out and touch the side of this great being, and you feel love and comfort radiating from it.

You stand still for a moment, soaking in the love and comfort. Now you move to stand before the Unicorn and gaze into its eyes. It moves its horn to the part of your body that most needs its energy, and you relax and receive.

You feel the Unicorn's energy weaving beautiful energy patterns within and around you, and you begin to sense that you are more than you were before. You stand and receive this energy, becoming one with it and the Unicorn.

Open your heart completely to your Guardian Unicorn, and go with it now on an inner journey. Allow a scene to unfold in your imagination, and if it feels right, follow along in your mind.

When you are ready, come back to the place filled with light and ask your Guardian Unicorn to help you create the day before you.

Imagine your Guardian Unicorn at your side as you see yourself going through the rest of your day, experiencing what you would love to experience, and feeling how you would love to feel.

Now take a deep breath and come back to your normal waking state, remembering the Unicorn at your side and the Unicorns all around you. Know that you are calling more of them into this reality with your attention and your love.

EVENING UNICORN MEDITATION

Allow the Unicorns to uplift your life even more by partnering with them as you sleep.

Tune in to the energy of your own heart, and feel Source love dwelling within it. Feel Source love spreading out from your heart to fill up your bedroom.

Fill yourself up with this Source love as you lie in your bed. Feel it filling the whole building with the energy of peace and safety.

Now feel the beautiful presence of your Guardian Unicorn standing by your bed. Feel the shimmering energy of the moon shining down on you, bathing you in its beauty and its light, and feel the connection between you and your Guardian Unicorn becoming stronger.

See luminous rainbow energy spiraling forth from your Guardian Unicorn's horn, creating a beautiful, safe energetic space within which you will sleep. Feel the love in your heart expand as you breathe in this rainbow light.

Say thank you to your Guardian Unicorn, knowing that your dreams and your life will be blessed by the love of this great being.

CREATE AN ONGOING UNICORN CONNECTION

Every time you remember the presence of the Unicorns, you raise your own energy and the energy of whatever situation you find yourself in.

Set an intention to imagine a Guardian Unicorn beside every person you meet today. Anchor in this intention by mentally reviewing the people you engaged with yesterday. One by one, call them forth in your mind, and imagine them with their Guardian Unicorns beside them.

Now imagine the coming day, and "see" Guardian Unicorns beside every person you plan to meet today.

As you go through your day, feel the Unicorns in front of you, behind you, and on either side of you. Start asking for help with everything you do.

Whenever you hear of a problem, whether in your life or in the world, imagine Unicorns repairing and uplifting the situation's energy field. If you are so guided, call forth Unicorns to raise the vibration of the government of your nation and of every nation.

See them creating new patterns, and help anchor in those patterns with your own intention and love.

We call always to the Unicorns.
Stay in our awareness
so that we may know you
and work alongside you
as you joyfully uplift
the energy of this world.
Be our Guardians and companions
as we journey through life, and please
repair,
upgrade,
and maintain
our personal energy fields,
so that we may live
as our best,
most radiant,
and most powerfully beautiful selves.

CHAPTER 3

MEET YOUR
ANGELIC GUARDIANS

Angel Invocation
We call upon the Angels:
champions of our destinies,
holders of the sacred keys,
keepers of the flame in our souls.
May we call upon you in all things
and align with your instruction
to create,
to uplift,
and to refashion this world.

In this chapter we'll be immersing ourselves in the Angelic energy that surrounds us and creating beautiful relationships with the Angels who can powerfully support us in our daily lives.

I'm going to invite you to open your heart to an understanding of Angels not only as living, loving beings, but also as *energy fields*. I'm also going to ask that you resist the urge to project human qualities onto Angelic Beings, because this limits what our relationships with them can be.

Angels are the holders of patterns.

Your Guardian Angel, for example, is the being *and* the energy field that holds the pattern for your best and fullest potential in this lifetime. Connecting with your Guardian Angel brings you into alignment with your unique divine blueprint—the blueprint that contains the best fulfillment of everything that's inside of you, waiting to be expressed.

Take in a nice fresh breath and let it out slowly, and as you do, open your heart to connect with your own Guardian Angel. Feel its presence within you and all around you, and open to its guidance and nourishing love.

Go deeply within yourself until you feel yourself in a beautiful room filled with golden light. Soak in the love you feel here, and let it fill and enliven every part of you.

Close your inner eyes as this beautiful energy continues to fill your being, and when you open them, realize that your Guardian Angel has taken the form of this room. As you stand within this room, you are enveloped within the love, support, and guidance of your own Guardian Angel.

Look around this beautiful room. What do you see or feel or sense as you stand in this sacred place that was created to support you on your life's path?

If it feels right, ask your Guardian Angel to take another form now. Commune with this beautiful being for as long as you like, feeling the power of your original divine blueprint being activated within you.

When you are ready, thank your Guardian Angel and close your inner eyes once more. When you open them, you find yourself back in your physical surroundings.

Take a deep breath and ground yourself into the love of the Earth as you come fully back to your normal waking state, feeling yourself fully in your body, and feeling the truth and power of your Guardian Angel still with you and all around you.

Thank your Guardian Angel and continue feeling its presence as you go through your day—and know that I am sending you love and thanking you for the beauty and power of the divine blueprint you bring with you into the world.

TAPPING INTO DIVINE ENERGY FIELDS

When you align your life force with the Angels' perfect patterns, your life begins to work in a powerful new way. So from now on, try to think of Angels not only as divine beings, but also as divine energy fields that you can tap into—and be enveloped within—whenever you choose.

I was so excited several years ago to come across the work of William Bloom. His book *Working with Angels, Fairies & Nature Spirits* gave form to my instinctive inner feelings and thoughts about Angels, and I am grateful for his teachings, some of which you will find reflected here through my own lens.

A simple—but life-changing—practice is to recognize the presence of Angels in the corners of every room you occupy.

Connect to the energy of your heart, and take a moment to get a sense of the energy of the room or space you currently occupy.

Now open yourself to the presence of four Angels, one in each corner of your room. You may perceive them as glowing beings, shining pillars of light, or in another form.

Take another moment and get a sense of the energy in the room now. Turn your focus inward and notice what you feel in your body now that you are surrounded by Angelic love.

Go a step further and imagine Angels in the four corners of every room in the house or building you are currently within. Do this one at a time, room by room, until every space is filled with Angelic love and light.

One last time, check in with your body, your emotions, and the energy around you. What changes do you feel?

Make this an ongoing practice, a habit that you repeat every time you enter a room. The Angelic energy filling each room will bless and uplift not only you but also everyone who enters.

THE GUARDIAN ANGEL OF YOUR HOME

No matter where you live, there is a Guardian Angel filling the space, and when you create a relationship with this Angel, it can support you in a powerful way. This is true whether you own your home, are renting, or are living in what you consider to be someone else's home.

This Angelic energy can support you in a multilayered way, through the Guardian Angel of the specific building you live in and through the overlighting Angel of all homes.

Sit quietly for a moment and tune in to the energy of your home. Notice what it feels like.

Now connect to your heart and silently greet the Angel of this space. Appreciation and love are the keys that will help you make connections with all Guardian Beings, so get into a place of appreciation for the Angel of your home. Thank it for its presence and notice what you feel in return.

Become aware now of how important your home is to your well-being, and allow yourself to feel a sense of love for the space around you. When you love your home, it will love you back, and that love will surround you and uplift you on an ongoing basis.

I often pat the walls of my house (and even kiss them sometimes). You don't have to go *that* far, but consider beginning the habit of greeting your house with love whenever you enter. (I like to say, "Hello, beautiful house" or "Hello, magical house.")

This is so simple to do, and the energy it creates is magical! Begin connecting in your own way starting today.

GUARDIAN SPIRITS OF CONVEYANCES

Now let's focus on the Angelic Guardians of the conveyances we use most often.

Whether you drive a car, ride a bike, or use public transportation, there's a Guardian Angel connected to each specific vehicle you use, as well as an overlighting Guardian connected to all vehicles of its type.

Tap into your heart energy right now and tune in to the Guardian Angel of the conveyance you use most often.

If it's your car, you may be able to feel the love it has for you. Open your heart to that love, and let it fill you and surround you. Imagine you are in the car, surrounded by that love, and say thank you. Begin a practice of connecting to the Guardian Angel of the car before and during each drive.

If you take the bus or train, you may notice that the energy you feel differs from one particular vehicle or train car to another. Tune in to the overlighting Guardian Angel of all the train cars or buses run by the organization that operates them.

Can you feel a sense of love, protectiveness, and purpose that comes through these vehicles from their Guardian Spirit? Connect to this Angel and say thank you right now, and again before each ride.

Once you're aboard a particular vehicle, thank the Guardian Angel who watches over it specifically, and give this Angel your blessing, that it may continue to help this vehicle carry people safely and happily to their destinations. (I especially love to do this on airplanes!)

LAYER UPON LAYER OF ANGELIC ENERGY

As we build layer upon layer of Angelic energy into our lives, it's important to include connecting to the Angel of our workplace, or the place where we spend the most time every day.

If you spend most of your day in your home, you might think that we've already covered this. But let's go deeper and connect to an *additional* layer of Angelic support.

First let's start with workplaces that are outside the home. If this applies to you, picture your workplace. Now connect to the Guardian Angel of the business you work for (this applies to your own business as well). If you work for a large company, you may be distracted by the energies and actions of the people who work in and with the business, but look past that to the actual Angelic energy at the core of the endeavor.

Angels are organizing intelligences, always holding a pattern of the potential of highest good, so even if the people working for or running your company are less than perfect, you can tap into something powerful and pure when you connect to its Guardian Angel.

Give this Guardian Spirit your blessing, and feel the energy of harmony and inspired purpose filling the rooms of your workplace.

If you are unemployed or retired, tap into the sense of purpose that fuels your days, and locate in your mind the place where you spend the most time during the day. Connect to the Guardian Spirit that connects that space to your soul purpose, and feel the space being filled with power and uplifting energy.

THE GUARDIAN ANGEL OF YOUR FAMILY

Now we'll connect to the Guardian Angel of your family of origin. This is one of my favorite things to do, and like everything, it gets easier and more rewarding with practice.

Each of us has a unique set of family members, so adapt these words to fit your particular situation. I like to start by picturing my parents and the house I grew up in, but not everyone has happy memories of growing up, so use your inner guidance as you go through this process.

Relax and connect through your heart to the Angelic presence that has been sending continual love to you and your family. If it helps, you can imagine this Angelic force above the center of your family home, radiating love and care to every person in your family, as it uplifts and harmonizes the connections between family members.

No matter where you are physically, try connecting to this Angel right now, and consciously connect to it whenever you think about or interact with members of your family.

This will support the energy of your heart and bring you a sense of peace and calm that might have been missing if there's been a lot of conflict in your family. I like to connect to the Angel of my family before I'm going to visit with them. And then, if things aren't going smoothly, I remember my connection, and it helps so much!

THE GUARDIAN ANGELS OF YOUR RELATIONSHIPS

I believe there's a Guardian Angel holding the pattern for the highest potential of each of our relationships. When we recognize and tap into the energy of these Angels, we allow our relationships to evolve into new levels of harmony and love.

Imagine Angels in the four corners of the room or space around you. This is now sacred space, and within this sacred space, imagine someone you know is standing in front of you.

Allow yourself to feel a beautiful rose-pink energy all around, supporting you both in its wonderful, nourishing energy. Now open your heart to the Guardian Angel of this relationship.

Feel the presence of the Guardian Angel of this relationship all around you both now. Feel yourself fully in your body as you do this, and allow the energy of this Guardian Angel to surround you both, nourishing and supporting each one of you as it supports your relationship together.

Focus now on the love you have for this person, and feel that love connecting you to this Guardian Angel. Feel the energy of this Guardian Spirit empowering both of you and the relationship, and feel the love of the Angels in the four corners of the room again.

When you are ready, come back into your normal waking state, and allow yourself to stay connected to this beautiful Guardian Angel.

Know that its energy will continue to support both of you in more and more wonderful ways as you continue to tap into it, open your heart, and thank it for its presence in your life.

Remember that every relationship in your life has its own Guardian Angel, watching over it, holding the pattern for its best fulfillment, and loving you both.

THE GUARDIAN ANGEL OF YOUR CITY, TOWN, OR VILLAGE

Now let's connect to the Guardian Angel of your city, town, or village.

Sit for a moment with the awareness that this Angel exists and that it's always there, continually pouring love and life force into the place you live.

It is also holding the pattern for the best unfolding of life within your town or city.

To connect to the Guardian Angel of your city, imagine yourself in the place you consider to be the "heart" of the city. (To make it easier, I'm going to simply refer to the place you live as a "city" from now on.)

Feel yourself sitting in this place, feeling fully in your body and grounded to the Earth, and connect to your own heart. Now open your heart to connect to the Angel of your city. Sense its presence in whichever way feels most natural to you. (You'll know you are on the right track when you feel more love in your heart.)

Now, holding in your awareness the presence of this Guardian Spirit, focus your attention on the Trees, the flowers, or some other feature in the landscape, and feel your own love for them.

As you do this, thank the Angel of the city.

Continue doing this for everything you see around you, including the cars, the buildings, and the people. Feel the love and wisdom of the Angel of the city shining into everyone and everything, and feel yourself at one with it.

When you feel complete, say thank you and set an intention to strengthen and expand your relationship with this beautiful being.

By focusing with love on what Guardian Beings love, you bring yourself into resonance with them, and by thanking them with your true, heartfelt appreciation, you create a bond that serves you, the Guardian Beings, and everyone in the world.

Continue to connect with the Angel of your city, and know that you can connect in this same way with the Guardian Spirits of every place you visit or travel through, feeling love and support no matter where you go.

ANGELIC PATTERNS

For every human undertaking, there is an Angelic pattern for the highest and best expression of the endeavor. So whatever it is that you want to be or do or have, there's an Angelic Being (a presence and a pattern all rolled into one) that you can call upon, connect with, and be enveloped within.

Your life force and your energy can join with this Angelic pattern and be uplifted and supported by it, to bring about the experience you're seeking in the best possible way.

Stop and really think of the many things you do in a day. Bring a few of them to mind now, one by one, knowing there is an Angel to support you with each one.

Open your heart to these Angels in this moment, and notice what you feel.

Once you become aware of and start actively engaging with the Guardian Energies all around you, nothing is ever the same, and the Angels will support you over and over as you move through this book.

I hope you'll begin to feel a new sense of connection, support, and love as you connect to the Guardian Angels in your life and share the power of your blessing with them.

We call upon the Angels:
champions of our destinies,
holders of the sacred keys,
keepers of the flame in our souls.
May we call upon you in all things
and align with your beauty
to create,
to uplift,
and to refashion this world.

CHAPTER 4

MEET YOUR TREE GUARDIANS

Tree Invocation

We call on the Trees
and we make a vow
from our hearts now:
to see you with new eyes,
to know you as treasured friends,
and to connect
through your roots
to the love
at the heart of this world.

You know that old saying, "Bloom where you're planted"? Some of us have never fully planted ourselves in the Earth realm. Instead, we've focused our spiritual energy on rising above physicality and the difficulties of the world.

But by creating true friendships with the Trees, you plant yourself in the physical world like never before. In doing so, you fully invest yourself here, creating a love affair with the nurturing energy of the Earth, while bringing through you all your spiritual power.

The Trees help us do this with the never-ceasing energy of love and wisdom they radiate.

27

Take a moment now and, if you can, look outside your window at a Tree. Tune out every distraction, until all you perceive is the Tree and you. Open your heart and accept the love the Tree has for you. Give it your love in return.

Trees are conscious, sentient beings who act as Guardians and wisdom-keepers for all life on Earth. We are dependent upon the Trees in more ways than we know, and it's time for us to live in *conscious* partnership with these great beings.

YOUR CHILDHOOD TREE

If I ask you to remember a Tree from your childhood, what comes to mind? When I first wrote this, I was expecting to bring the image of a weeping willow to my mind, because that was the first Tree I remember from my childhood.

But what came to my mind instead was the sycamore Tree that stands in the front yard of my parents' house. We moved into this house when I was four years old, and my parents lived there for over fifty years. I grew up in the energy field of this Tree.

I think of it now like a beautiful Grandmother Tree watching over my whole family, and I love and appreciate it so much!

When you think of a Tree from your childhood, you may think of a Tree that's no longer physically present, or you may not remember a specific Tree. Either way, allow a Tree to come into your mind now, and as you do, allow your own energetic roots to go deeply down into the Earth.

As your roots go down, see them moving to connect to the roots of this Tree from your childhood. See the roots intertwining in mutual love and support. Now connect to the energy of your heart and imagine that this Tree from your childhood also has an energetic heart. Allow yourself to form a bond between these two hearts.

Stay present to this bond and be strengthened and supported by the love you share with this beautiful Tree Being.

YOUR GUARDIAN TREE

Now let's take a journey together to connect to a personal Tree Guardian.

> *Relax into your deepest self, drop energetic roots down into the Earth, and allow yourself to connect through your heart to the energy of the Trees. As you do, feel the energy of deep, steady love all around you, and within this love feel the presence of a personal Tree Guardian.*

> *Welcome this beautiful being in whatever way it appears to you. Feel its branches arching protectively over you, and in your mind's eye, feel a deep heart connection taking place.*

> *Feel the warm, steady love this Tree feels for you, and give yourself some time to commune with this beautiful being.*

> *When you're ready, thank this Tree for its presence in your life. See yourself giving a special gift to your Guardian Tree and feel its thanks.*

> *As you go through the rest of your day, consciously connect to the energy of your own heart and feel the presence of your Guardian Tree there.*

BEGIN WHERE OTHERS HAVE PAVED THE WAY

I used to live in a neighborhood where all the front yards had several Trees. I took a morning walk through the neighborhood every day, and as I did, I began to notice that even though I appreciated *all* the Trees, I felt drawn to some and not others.

Even though there were two beautiful mimosa Trees on my walk, only one of them felt magical to me. Of the many flowering fruit Trees that grew, a certain pair always caught my attention.

And there was one Tree that stood out most of all: a towering Cedar Pine Tree. I felt such a wonderful energy coming from that Tree that I made sure to linger and send it love as I walked by. The pine cones from this Tree looked like tiny wooden roses, and I picked one up every time I walked by so I could keep a part of the Tree with me.

One day as I was passing, I saw a woman in the yard watering flowers. I stopped and said, "I love your Tree!"

She smiled and said, "We do, too!"

That's when it hit me. Maybe the reason I could easily feel a heart connection with some Trees was that other humans had paved the way, creating a relationship with each Tree through their affection for it.

I now noticed that two adorable little girls played in the yard with the two flowering Trees, and I imagined that the people who lived with the magical mimosa Tree were probably connecting with *it* in some way.

I believe that with patience, persistence, and love you can make friends with any Tree in the world. But look around your neighborhood, open your heart to the Trees you see, and notice if any of them seem to stand out to you.

From now on, say a special hello and send love to these Trees every time you pass by. Allow a relationship to grow and deepen through your consistent, loving attention.

In this way, you'll take a new place in the spiritual ecosystem of your neighborhood, becoming part of a beautiful energetic network that will support both you and the Trees you befriend.

DEVELOP A DEEPER FRIENDSHIP

Now let's choose one Tree to develop a deeper friendship with.

Let your heart guide you, and pick a Tree you'll be able to visit on a daily basis.

Once you've chosen a Tree, the first step is just to sit quietly with the Tree for a few minutes. Ground yourself into the love of the Earth, feel Source love filling your being, and turn inward to get a clear sense of your own energy.

Then greet the Tree and open yourself to its energy. Thank it for its presence and tell it all the things you appreciate about it (this can be done silently).

Gently hold your palm against its trunk, close your eyes, and open your heart. Notice any impressions or feelings that come to you as you commune with this new friend.

Now thank the Tree, pat its trunk, and get ready to say goodbye for today. Look around on the ground and see if there's anything you feel you have permission to take with you.

This process doesn't have to take a long time, but if you spend a few moments every day communing with the Tree in this way, a relationship will grow in its own unique, beautiful way.

SURROUNDED BY FRIENDS

Making friends with even one Tree creates a bond between you and the overlighting Spirit of all Trees, and as you encounter new Trees, you'll be able to feel the energy of that bond.

Soon after I discovered this, my friend Glennie took me out to lunch in the seaside city of Carmel (two hours away) to celebrate my birthday. The road we traveled on had Trees on either side, and as we drove, I told her about my new relationship with the Trees.

"Look," I said. "We have friends all around us, and we don't even realize it!"

Today, begin a new way of moving in the world, connected to the loving presence of the Trees. When you wake in the morning, greet the overlighting Spirit of all Trees with love and thanks. Think for a moment about the Trees growing around the world and send them all love.

Connect to the presence of your Guardian Tree and take its love and wisdom with you into the day.

Send a special greeting to the Trees in your city or town, and spend a moment feeling at one with them. As you travel to neighboring cities or towns, connect to the Trees there and greet them with love and appreciation.

You are literally *surrounded* by friends in the form of the Trees. Make that friendship part of your life starting today.

TAKE YOUR PLACE AMONG THE TREES

Taking a journey to the forest within can help you become one with the Trees in a deeper way, and this deep connection will strengthen and support the beauty and power within you.

Connect to the love of the Earth and allow yourself to go deeply within. Go deeper and deeper until you find yourself standing in a beautiful forest.

Sunlight shines through the Trees, and you can feel magic all around you.

There are Trees of all kinds in this forest, and before you stands your own Guardian Tree. Place your hand lovingly upon its trunk, and feel love and peace pouring into you.

Keeping your hand on the trunk of the Tree, look around and feel the same steady, ongoing love coming from every Tree in the forest—and every Tree in the world.

Lean against your Guardian Tree and take in this love. Feel yourself grounded by this love and able to feel your own energetic roots growing deeply into the Earth.

Now feel your energy spreading high into the sky, and allow yourself to feel a deep, deep sense of support in your legs, hips, stomach, chest—and every part of your body.

Think back to your childhood and remember a special Tree that grew near to where you lived. Know that even if you can't remember a special Tree, it was there just the same.

This Tree was a Guardian, watching over you and acting as a continual source of love and support. Connect with the energy of that Guardian Tree now and feel the power of its love coming to you across the years.

Recognize that you also have a physical Guardian Tree now, near the home where you live or the place where you work.

In truth, all Trees are your loving Guardians, but one Tree in particular has a special love for you. Allow the image of this Tree to come into your mind, and thank it.

Allow this heart connection to go both ways from now on, and create an ongoing relationship with all your Guardian Trees.

Take in a deep breath, and as you do, breathe in the love of all the Trees and thank them for their presence in the world.

Take your time coming back into your normal waking state. Move around a bit, feel yourself fully in your body, and allow the love of the Trees to awaken and energize you.

Move back into the physical world feeling part of a magical forest. Once you make friends with the Trees, you are never alone, and you yourself will begin to blossom!

MAKE TREE FRIENDS WHEN YOU TRAVEL

Once you establish a practice of greeting Trees as you travel through neighboring cities or towns, take your practice a step further and make friends with the Trees you meet while traveling.

A few years ago, I stayed at a hotel during a three-day business conference. I love events like this, but I've learned to take lots of breaks to go back to my room and recharge.

On this particular trip, I noticed a beautiful Pine Tree growing right outside my hotel room window. I said hello, sent it appreciation and love, and felt grateful that I had a Tree friend to connect with during my stay.

I moved a comfy chair close to the window, and on my breaks from the conference I took several minutes to relax, commune with the Tree, and recenter myself. The Tree was very easy to connect with, and (as usually happens) I felt from it a sense of happiness for the appreciation I was sending its way.

Remember this idea and put it into action the next time you go on a trip. Even better, start making friends this way with the Trees outside your favorite restaurants or the place you work.

Love is the master key that allows you to communicate with any being. Using the key of love will help you connect to more and more Trees as you move through the world.

BECOME ONE WITH A SACRED GROVE

I always feel a lot of support and help from Guardian Beings when I create my telesummits, but when I hosted my *Tree Spirit Telesummit* a few years ago, there was a noticeable difference.

When I first began creating the telesummit, my intention was to help people create deeper relationships with the Trees around them, but as I listened to each speaker, I saw there was a greater intention at work. There were Tree connections and activations taking place that went far beyond what I'd originally hoped for when I created the event.

I felt the energy of a sacred grove of Trees coming forth to bless the event and hold special energetic space for the telesummit listeners, the speakers, and me. As the telesummit progressed I felt the sacred grove getting larger, with more and more Trees coming forward.

I felt them in the room with me as I hosted each call, and I'd like to invite you to feel their presence with you now with a daily Tree Communion Practice:

Go within and see the whole planet held in a space of safety and love.

Now feel yourself entering a sacred grove, filled with Trees that have come forward to hold this sacred space with us.

Feel yourself become centered within this grove. Feel yourself become grounded. Feel yourself become balanced. Within this sacred grove, feel yourself become whole.

Feel yourself in loving partnership with the energies of life all around you, and open your heart fully to the spirits of the Trees.

Connect with love to the Trees that are physically near you at this moment. Feel their steady, supportive presence all around you, and feel your own energetic roots connecting you to their roots.

Set an intention to create a beautiful relationship with the spirits of the Trees around you, wherever you go.

Staying grounded into the Earth, shine love from your heart to all the Trees in your city or town. Feel your own energetic roots connecting you to their roots. Now open your heart to receive any energy or communication you feel coming from them.

Shine love to all the Trees in your state or province. Feel your own energetic roots connecting you to their roots. Open your heart to receive any energy or communication you feel coming from them.

Shine love to all the Trees on your continent, and open your heart to receive any energy or communication you feel coming from them. Feel your energetic roots connecting you to their roots.

Shine love to all the Trees in your hemisphere, and open your heart to receive any energy or communication you feel coming from them. Feel your energetic roots connecting you to their roots.

Now shine your love to all the Trees across the planet, feeling your energetic roots connecting you to their roots. Feel their love in return, and become part of a beautiful, interconnected pattern of love and support.

Feel your own beautiful energy once again, come back to your own heart, and thank the Trees who have come forth to bring their energy to your life and the world.

Feel yourself in vibrant, powerful partnership with all the Trees, and take your place in the creative tapestry of life that we are weaving together.

The Trees have been creating expanding networks of connection that go beyond our one-on-one connections, and when you bring your focus to them and consistently connect to them with love, you support them in their work.

And they will support you in more ways than you will ever know.

Once we become aware of Trees as conscious beings, the way we move through the world changes. In the chapters that follow, the Trees will help and support you as you learn how to create a foundation of self-love, trust yourself, be open to receive, and reclaim your spark.

As this chapter comes to a close, we return to our Tree invocation, this time with love and thanks born of our new, deeper connection with the Trees.

We thank the Trees with love
and we make a vow
from our hearts now:
to see you with new eyes,
to know you as treasured friends,
and to connect
through your roots
to the love
at the heart
of this world.

CHAPTER 5

MEET THE EARTH SOUL

Earth Invocation

We call upon the Earth
and we say thank you.
Thank you for powering
this world in which we live,
sustaining it with your love
and your spirit.
May we come into alignment
with the beauty that surrounds us—
beauty you create and sustain
through the power of your love.

The Earth is not just what's below our feet. It's the biosphere we live within.

Look out a window. Everything you see is held in place and supported by the Guardian Being that is the Earth. We don't just live *on* the Earth; we actually live *in* it.

The Earth feels to me like a gigantic Guardian Angel that I live inside of—a Guardian Being that nourishes and supports all life.

As you move through this book, it's my hope that you'll learn how to deepen your own experience of the Earth as a living, conscious being—and that you'll begin to have your own personal, unique relationship with that being.

Let's begin by connecting with the Earth in a mundane yet powerful way.

If you can scoop up a handful of dirt, do it now, and if you can't, then scoop up a handful of dirt in your imagination. First feel the texture of the Earth between your fingers.

Now go deeper, and tune in to the energetic signature of the Earth in your hand. When I do this, I automatically feel a heart connection spring forth. If you haven't already, connect through your heart to this Earth in your hand.

Hold it to your heart, and come into attunement with it. Let your new relationship with this piece of Earth extend to all the soil covering the planet.

Now, either physically or in your mind's eye, place the Earth with great care in a special spot on the ground outside.

Set an intention to remain in attunement with the Earth in the form of this soil, and let this new relationship support you and bring you comfort every time you think of it.

THE SACRED BALANCE OF EARTH

Part of being connected to the Earth is staying aware of your own patterns and rhythms. When you wake up in the morning, what are your first thoughts? Do you feel fully in your body, or are you in a somewhat disconnected state?

Take a deep breath now, and as you do, connect to the physicality of your body.

Feel the energy and love of the Earth in your feet, in your lower legs, in your thighs, in your pelvis, in your abdomen, in your chest, in your shoulders, in your arms, in your hands, in your neck, and in your head.

Feel the energy of the Earth in every part of your being. What does it feel like to you?

Turn your attention inward, and tune in to your own internal patterns. How does the energy within your body naturally want to flow?

The Earth is literally the stable foundation we stand on, but it is also a flowing, dynamic presence that we can align with to reach a state of balance within ourselves. Connect to the living presence of the Earth within you now, and allow your body to come into a state of sacred balance.

Return to this state of balance as often as possible, and remember that the Earth (and I) are always sending you love!

CONNECT TO THE EARTH'S LOVE

Now let's talk about the energy of Earth that is found in all physical matter. We'll start with a question: How do you feel about being in a physical body?

For that matter, what is your relationship with your body? It seems like so much spiritual conversation centers on trying to transcend the body and physical form. But I believe we incarnated here on purpose and for an important reason.

Instead of trying to escape physical form and return to your nonphysical spiritual self, I believe in working toward bringing more and more of your spiritual essence into your physical form and your Earthly experience. We do this (as with so many things!) by using the power of love, and it starts by connecting with the love that comes to us from the Spirit of Earth.

Allow yourself to feel a beam of Source love entering through the top of your head. Let this energy flow down into your body, through your feet, and down to the center of the Earth. At the center of the Earth, feel once more the presence of a huge glowing crystal, filled with positive energy and love.

See the beam of Source love flow down into the crystal, harmonize with the Earth's love there, and beam straight back up into you. Feel this beautiful love energy filling your heart and spreading out all around you until it encompasses the whole world.

Feel yourself at one with the energy of the Earth, at one with the matter that makes up your body, and at one with the Spirit that flows through it.

Feel the Earth supporting you as you let the love from your own heart flow out and take shape around you. See yourself creating more and more of what you love in your life, and feel the Earth's love supporting you in bringing your divine gifts into physical form.

When you're ready, come back to your normal waking state, and allow the power within the Earth's love to activate and energize every cell in your body as you move through the world.

MAKE FRIENDS WITH A MOUNTAIN

When I was four years old, my family moved to the city of Concord, California, which is located in the Diablo Valley, named for our mountain, Mount Diablo. Pretty much wherever we go in Concord, the twin peaks of this beautiful mountain can be seen.

Its image is found in the city's logo and in numerous business names and graphics (I even went to school in the Mt. Diablo Unified School District). When I see this mountain, I know I'm home.

All my life, this beautiful mountain has been watching over me, but only in recent years did I awaken to its living presence.

I live a short distance from Concord now, and I have a different view of the mountain. I'm looking at it from my desk as I write, and I connect with it continuously every day as I work.

Its presence has been a real blessing in my life, and today I invite you to open your heart and create a loving friendship with the mountain of your choice.

(If you live in an area with no mountains present, don't worry. Your relationship with the Earth is present wherever you are, and it connects you to all the other parts of it. Just let a particular mountain come into your mind, and create a connection with it, even if it is far away.)

Let a mountain come into your mind now. Look at the actual mountain or a picture, or just imagine it in your mind. Greet it with reverence, and thank it for its presence.

Now open your heart to commune with this mountain. (You may not feel anything at first. Just give it time, and with repeated contact you'll begin to feel more and more of a heart connection.)

Feel yourself connected to this mountain not only through your heart, but also through the ground under your feet that connects you.

Feel at one with this beautiful being. Notice what you feel in your body and emotions now.

When you feel complete, thank the mountain again. You may feel (as I do) that a piece of this mountain is now within your heart.

Remember the majestic, powerful presence of this mountain as you go through your day, and align yourself with its energy to feel more stable, grounded, and empowered.

THE SPIRIT OF THE EARTH IN OBJECTS

How many times have you felt alone on your path? It's easy to feel cut off from the support and nurturing that each one of us needs every day, so it's time to lift the veil and recognize the Spirit of Earth in the things around us.

I believe every "thing" has its own consciousness, and that includes the things we consider to be inanimate objects. I also believe that the consciousness of each thing is on its own journey of evolution. (We'll be going into this subject in depth in Chapter 24.)

In addition to its other energies, every physical thing around you also contains the Spirit of Earth.

That means that the same loving, nurturing energy that you feel when you ground into the Earth under your feet can also be found within the physical objects around you.

Stop and really take this in. Look around and notice the objects that surround you. Really see each thing, and as you do, tune in to the Earth energy within it.

Can you feel the loving presence within the physical form of each thing? Soak it in, and let it uplift you. Then bless each thing with your love.

The energies in the objects around us are made up of many things, but the Spirit of the Earth is always present in each one.

As you go through your day today, set aside a few moments throughout the day to notice the things around you and connect to the love of the Earth in each one. Make this a regular, supportive ritual, a habit that will help you consciously connect to the Earth's loving energy.

THE TABLE OF LIFE

The Earth knows and loves you, and it wants you to thrive and flourish.

Tune in to your own energy field, and call all your energy back into your body. Drop energetic roots down into the Earth, and feel love and support flowing up to envelop you. Focus on the energy of your own heart, and feel your own beautiful "energy signature."

Now imagine life as a banquet. In your mind's eye, see a beautiful banquet table stretching out in both directions farther than the eye can see, and see before you your place at the table.

See a place card with your name on it, and allow yourself to take your rightful place there. Seated at this table, you see that it's not just a place to receive the Earth's bounty, but also a place to share your own gifts. Your place at the table can only be filled by you.

Now expand your awareness to see the whole Earth as a beautiful "table." See the place card with your name on it everywhere you look, and feel the Earth Soul enveloping you in its nurturing love.

Allow your heart to fill with this love, and make it a part of you from now on. Feel yourself part of the Earth's heart, and know how precious you are.

TAKE YOUR PLACE ON THE EARTH

We'll end this chapter by connecting to the Earth in a deep and personal way.

Once more, allow yourself to feel a beautiful beam of Source energy entering through the top of your head. As this Source energy flows down into your body, feel it cleansing, clearing, and balancing every part of your body and every part of your being.

Draw in more and more of this pure Source life force. Feel it filling your entire body, flowing through your feet, and beaming down into the center of the Earth. At the center of the Earth, feel the presence of a huge glowing crystal, filled with positive energy and love for you.

See the beam of Source energy flow down into the crystal, harmonize with the energy there, and beam straight back up into you. Feel this beautiful energy flow up in a gentle wave, a wave that fills you, surrounds you, and then spreads out to bless the entire world. See the whole planet held in a space of safety and love.

Now think of the roots of a magnificent Tree. Picture an abundant, healthy root system, and allow your own energetic roots to move down into the rich, fertile Earth beneath your feet.

Feel your roots spreading out and spiraling down, down, and further down . . . anchoring you into the love and nourishment of the Earth.

Draw that love and nourishment up now, and feel it filling your energetic roots and your body. Feel it completely filling your heart, and take a few minutes now to commune through your heart with the conscious being that is the Earth.

Now feel beautiful crystals and gemstones in the Earth beside your roots, supporting you with their powerful energy. Draw in more pure life-force energy from Source, and feel it shining from you, blessing and energizing the crystals around your roots and the Earth itself.

Feel the power of your root system, the power of having a solid home in and on the Earth: a place where you feel welcomed, nourished, and supported.

Finally, imagine your body as a magnificent Tree, supported by Guardian Beings, and see the fruits of your own gifts blossoming forth from your branches to bless the world.

Grounding into the love and support of the Earth will be a vital part of everything we do in the chapters to come, and I hope it will be a vital part of your daily life as well.

We call upon the Earth
and we say thank you.
Thank you for powering
this world in which we live,
sustaining it with your love
and your spirit.
May we stay in alignment
with the beauty that surrounds us—
adding to the beauty you create and sustain
through the power of your love.

PART II

TRANSFORM YOUR LIFE WITH THE HELP OF YOUR GUARDIANS

This Part will help you create a strong inner foundation and gain the skills you need to start living life in an expanded, empowered way. As a reminder, I suggest you read the chapters in order, and then you can return to the chapters with the skills you want to work on as needed. There are exercises and meditations throughout. You can complete them in your head, read them aloud, or write them down in a journal. For a richer, guided experience, you can get my *Guardian Gateway Activation Experience*, which contains 29 videos and more than 60 illustrated transformation sheets. (Visit www.kimwilborn.com/activation-experience for more information.)

CHAPTER 6

CREATE A FOUNDATION OF SELF-LOVE

Now that you've met your Guardians, it's time to make a change that will transform everything in your life: loving yourself.

I've come to believe that loving ourselves is a spiritual path in and of itself.

That seems too self-focused, doesn't it? But think of it this way: loving yourself brings you into alignment with the Guardian Beings who are waiting to help you fulfill your soul purpose.

If you're reading this book, I know you want to bring positive change to the world around you—either through the work you do or just through your way of "being" in the world. Learning how to actively, consistently engage with the energy of self-love will help you create a life that's aligned with your own soul purpose, a life that fits who you truly are on a deep level.

Loving yourself creates a strong foundation from which to bring your true heart's desires into being, and coming from that strong foundation of self-love will support and empower you in being a powerful force for good in the world.

Your self-talk will change, and you'll find yourself saying supportive things to yourself (more on this later!). You'll also receive powerful inspirations you've never had before.

Loving yourself opens doors you didn't even know were there.

In this chapter we'll talk about what loving yourself is, how you can make self-love the core of your life, and why it *needs* to be the core of your life right now.

You'll learn how to create an energetic space of love and power that uplifts you and everyone around you. The mindset shifts you'll experience—and the new behaviors you'll put into place—will cause a ripple effect that touches every part of your life.

TWO CAMPS

It seems like most of us fall into one of two camps when it comes to loving ourselves. Check in now and determine which describes you best: Does it feel just plain *wrong* to focus on loving yourself? Or does it feel right (intellectually, at least), but you don't know how to do it?

I can relate to both answers; I came to the subject of loving myself in a roundabout way.

A few years ago I created the *Guardian Spirits of Nature Telesummit* and interviewed 22 experts on the topic of partnering with Nature Beings of all kinds. This was one of my all-time favorite events, and there was one thing several speakers brought up: how important self-love is when it comes to connecting to the Guardian Spirits in nature (and Guardian Beings in general).

I instinctively felt this was true, but I'd never learned a method of self-love that brought a real change in me, so I put the idea on the back burner.

Then I had a breakthrough. I began to think of loving myself not in mental or psychological terms, but instead as a practice—a practice of engaging with the *living energy and life force* of love.

The self-love techniques I'd heard about in the past mostly had to do with changing my thoughts, like looking for things to like about myself or using affirmations. I'd tried these things, but there was still a huge difference between the love I felt for others and the love I felt for myself.

That difference showed up in the form of uncertainty, worry, and self-doubt, all energies that get in the way of sharing my gifts with the world.

My breakthrough came when I began to approach the subject of loving myself not from a mental standpoint, but instead by connecting to the *energy* of love.

What a difference! This felt like the missing piece in my own spiritual foundation.

When we're not loving ourselves, we are out of alignment with the flow of universal love and life force that's seeking to flow through us.

Loving ourselves gives us access to so much creative power.

So let's go back to the question of whether loving ourselves is wrong, and do a quick exercise.

Take a deep breath, let it out and relax, and bring to mind the last time you were in a restaurant.

Picture yourself walking into the restaurant, and imagine the other diners there, already seated when you walked in. Bring yourself back to this scene, and get a sense of how their energy feels.

Have you got it? Now imagine the exact same scene in the same restaurant, but this time, imagine that every single person there is actively engaged in loving themselves.

What do their faces look like now?

How does the space around them feel?

And how does this make you feel?

Experiencing this energy, even in your imagination, shows you how powerful it is and how much it blesses everyone around it. So I'm not going to try to convince you that you deserve to love yourself. Instead I'm going to say: *Just do it!*

Just decide to create a new habit of actively engaging in the energy of loving yourself. Do it without needing reasons why you're "worth it." Accept it as a task that will help you fulfill your soul purpose in this lifetime.

Make the decision to start actively engaging an energy of loving yourself, because you know that your spiritual empowerment depends on it.

THE "HOW" OF IT

Now we come to the most important part, the "how" of it all!

Try this: imagine that you're looking at someone or something that you love with an instinctive love, like a small child or your pet. You don't need a reason to love them, you "just do."

Get a sense of what that love feels like.

Now picture the love you feel as a big ball of energy, a sphere that surrounds the person or animal you love. Imagine that this energy is a beautiful transparent color, and see your loved one within this colored sphere, happily absorbing its energy.

This sphere is a manifestation of the living energy of love.

Let the ball of love expand now. Feel it getting bigger and bigger in your mind, until it reaches and includes you. Just sit and feel this energy for a moment, and notice what it feels like—without thinking about it.

Relax into the energy of love. Really soak it up. As you do, ground yourself into the love of the Earth, and feel yourself supported on all sides.

Over time, this instinctive flow of love can be an energy you naturally inhabit.

YOUR HOUSE OF SELF-LOVE

Everything is energy, and we harness the power to create when we unite our minds with our hearts. So in the rest of this chapter I'll give you three powerful energy practices you can use on an ongoing basis to connect to the energy of self-love.

The first practice is one that we'll refer to over and over again throughout this book: building a strong energetic home for yourself made from the energy of love.

Take a deep breath and allow your body to relax. Connect to Source love, and connect to the love the Earth has for you. Allow yourself to feel very welcomed in this physical world.

Remember the ball of love you created earlier in this chapter, and call it forth to surround you again. Now imagine that this ball of love is transforming itself into a sturdy energetic house that is building itself around you. This house is made of self-love—not your current state of self-love, but the self-love you are meant to have.

See this beautiful house build itself around you, and notice how it feels. Feel the house's foundation forming a strong energetic foundation under you, and feel the strength of that love holding and supporting you.

Feel the presence of ancient, wise Trees supporting both you and your house.

Now center yourself within this energy of love surrounding you, connect to your own heart energy, and say, "I love myself." (This may sound like just another affirmation, but it's actually the key to this house, so don't skip this part!)

This house can go with you everywhere you go. Allow yourself to feel cushioned by it and held safely within its living energy field of love.

Your house of self-love is a Gateway, a place of connection to the living energy field of love. By consistently imagining it around you, you stabilize your connection to the energy of love, and you become immersed in the energy field of love at all times.

With this house around you, you can grow and expand to your full potential.

This practice might seem too simple to make a real difference. But the energetic structure you are building is very real, and it will get stronger and more powerful with time.

The reason all the practices in this chapter are simple (and yet so effective) is that *loving yourself is actually how you are meant to be.*

Loving ourselves is our natural state, and if you doubt that, think back to our restaurant example. The energy of people who are loving themselves creates a beautiful energy field that supports and uplifts everyone around them.

I remind myself to feel my house of self-love around me every chance I get. I perceive my house as a kind of see-through structure surrounding me on all sides. When I catch myself worrying about something, I focus on my heart, say, "I love myself," and feel the energy of the house (and the ancient wise Trees) around me.

I'm instantly shifted and uplifted.

THE ANGEL OF PEACE

A lot of people feel that they *already* love themselves, but there's a big difference between thinking about love versus actively *engaging* in the energy of love.

For instance, my grown daughter, Jenny, moved in with me once for a few months while she was in between apartments. (She finally found a good apartment near the beach in San Francisco, and now I only get to see her when she drives the 90 minutes out to my house or I go into the city.)

Of course I love Jenny every minute of every day (if you're a parent, I know you can relate!), but when she moved in with me, I realized that there's a big difference in my energy when I am with her versus when we're apart.

I love her *all* the time, but when I am with her or talking to her on the phone—when I'm focusing on her—I am *actively* flowing love toward her.

We can apply this awareness to ourselves. Instead of just thinking about loving ourselves, we can choose to *actively engage* with the energy of self-love. This brings us to our second self-love practice, which has to do with self-acceptance.

It starts with the Angel of Peace. Soon after my breakthrough about how to love myself, I was doing some shopping at an outdoor mall. As I walked from one store to another, I noticed something different in the other shoppers. It was as if everyone was off balance in some way.

As I walked, I silently asked for a Guardian to help us all. Immediately I felt the presence of a Guardian energy I'd never felt before. The feeling was so powerful that I felt I had to stop what I was doing and walk back to my car.

Once there, I sat down in the passenger seat, closed my eyes, and opened my heart to the new Guardian energy that was suddenly all around me.

It was rich, deep-pink Angelic energy that made me feel like I was inside a loving womb, able to absorb everything I needed in order to heal and evolve.

It felt like being enveloped in a great Angel of Peace, and I knew in my heart that this Guardian was here for all of us.

Take a deep breath and slowly let it out. As you relax, allow yourself to welcome a sense of comfort in your body. Surround yourself with this feeling of comfort; breathe it in and feel yourself filled up with deep comfort.

Now focus your attention on the energy of your heart, and create a new space in your heart for self-acceptance. See this as an actual place you are creating—a temple of self-acceptance within your heart.

Feel the Angel of Peace filling this place in your heart with deep, rich, pink energy, and dedicate this space to self-acceptance. Set an intention to allow into this space everything about yourself that you've been rejecting. Allow these things to enter your heart one by one, and as they do, let them be transformed by the power of love.

Do this now. Let a part of yourself you've been rejecting come to mind. Now bring this part of yourself into the temple of self-acceptance you have created in your heart. Let it be held in this nurturing pink energy. How does it feel?

Set an intention to become aware whenever you're rejecting a part of yourself. Bring the thing you are about to reject into this energy of love within your heart, and feel yourself becoming more whole.

Know that your truth—the truth of being a force of powerful love, just as you are—is activating every part of your being now. Feel it alive within you, and feel the transforming power of love spread out to every part of your life.

It's important to remember that the self-love we're talking about isn't conditional. You have it all day long, no matter what happens.

I had a breakthrough on this subject about 10 years ago. For a long time before that, I'd wanted to become an officiant and perform weddings. For years I just played around with the idea and never took action on it, then two of my clients asked me if I would marry them.

Even though I'd taught and spoken in front of crowds many times, I'd never performed this kind of ceremony before. *This* was a really profound and sacred thing, and I was so nervous about doing it!

I put a ton of effort into creating a really beautiful ceremony, and I practiced and I practiced . . . but a few days before the ceremony, I was hit with a wave of overwhelming stage fright.

When I sat with the feeling of fear, it came to me that what I needed to do was to tell myself that even if I totally screwed up the ceremony, I wouldn't abandon myself.

No matter what, I would still love myself.

And that made all the difference. I actually didn't screw up (yay!), but the value in the story is not the outcome, but the shift that took place within me.

Promising not to abandon myself changed everything, and it made me aware of how often we abandon ourselves based on our performance. (No wonder we're scared to show up in the world!)

So begin telling yourself that you won't abandon yourself if you do poorly or if you screw up or if you embarrass yourself. Tell yourself that no matter what happens, you won't reject yourself— and really mean it!

This is no less than you would expect from a partner or a friend. It's actually what you *would* expect from someone who loves you, so start, right now, to give it to yourself.

We don't need to earn our own respect; we just need to not reject ourselves.

COLORS AND SELF-LOVE

Our third self-love practice calls on the living, healing energies of color. I'll outline the process using eight colors, but please feel free to build on this practice using any colors you like.

Take a deep breath, let it out slowly, and focus your attention on your body.

Breathe in the loving energy of the color red, and feel it fill you and surround you. Now choose a part of your body to come into your mind. It might be your stomach, your feet, your shoulders, your thigh muscles, or any other part of your body.

Let this chosen part of your body come into your consciousness. As you gently bring your focus to this part of yourself, say, "I love you."

Now breathe in the loving energy of the color orange, and feel it fill you and surround you. Let a different part of your body come into your mind, and bring your focus to this part of yourself. As you gently focus on this part of your body, say, "I love you."

Now breathe in the loving energy of the color yellow, and feel it fill you and surround you. Let a part of your body come into your mind, and bring your focus to this part of yourself. As you gently focus on this part of your body, say, "I love you."

Now breathe in the loving energy of the color green, and feel it fill you and surround you. Let a part of your body come into your mind, and bring your focus to this part of yourself. As you gently focus on this part of your body, say, "I love you."

Now breathe in the loving energy of the color blue, and feel it fill you and surround you. Let a part of your body come into your mind, and bring your focus to this part of yourself. As you gently focus on this part of your body, say, "I love you."

Now breathe in the loving energy of the color indigo, and feel it fill you and surround you. Let a part of your body come into your mind, and bring your focus to this part of yourself. As you gently focus on this part of your body, say, "I love you."

Now breathe in the loving energy of the color violet, and feel it fill you and surround you. Let a part of your body come into your mind, and bring your focus to this part of yourself. As you gently focus on this part of your body, say, "I love you."

Now breathe in loving white energy, and feel it fill you and surround you. Let a part of your body come into your mind, and bring your focus to this part of yourself. As you gently focus on this part of your body, say, "I love you."

Check in with yourself and notice how you feel emotionally and physically as you ground yourself into the love of the Earth.

I like to do this practice before I get out of bed in the morning. It's powerful at any time, but it's especially potent when done on a regular basis!

A NEW BEGINNING

The more love you feel, the more powerful you are. Think about that for a moment, and notice how it applies to your own life. To be a truly powerful force for good in the world, we have to extend the love we feel to include our own selves.

I hope you'll take the practices from this chapter and make them an important part of your life from now on. Use them as an antidote to the negative messages and a strong new foundation on which to fulfill your dreams.

I'm seeing you loving yourself, and I'm seeing your life changing in wondrous ways!

CHAPTER 7

❧

OPEN TO NEW POSSIBILITIES

It's easy to develop a kind of tunnel vision as we go through life. We tend to stay focused on the same old things (mostly things we think we have to do). But there are so many more possibilities out there! And the more possibilities you are open to, the more easily your life can be improved, uplifted, and transformed.

In this chapter we'll join together to relax any rigid thought patterns you have concerning what is possible for you, and you'll learn how to open your mind to allow your good to come to you in more and more ways.

We'll create space for you to open to new insights, new ideas, and new discoveries, broadening your inner landscape to include a wealth of magical possibilities you haven't known until now.

We'll expand and strengthen your inner landscape so you can step into new possibilities with a sense of wholeness and power, and we'll start by creating space for new inspiration to enter.

Think of something you'd like to experience. Now think of the path you believe you have to travel in order to have this experience. (Another way of saying this is: think of your current plan to get the thing you want.)

Think of your current plan like a path, stretching out before you. Get a sense of this path in your mind, and see the thing or experience you want waiting at the end of the path.

We usually think we have to follow our plan and make our way down the path to finally get to the thing we want. We see a big space between ourselves and the thing or experience we want to have, and we usually see one main way to go about getting it.

But today let's take a deep breath and get in receptive mode instead. Think of the path before you and your beliefs about what you have to do to get to the prize at the end. Now reverse the direction of the path, so that you see the thing you want traveling up the path toward you.

See the thing you want being drawn to you, and open your heart to receive it.

Now see 10 more paths appear around you—all leading toward you. You are at the center of all of these paths with the thing you want to have or be or do coming toward you on every one of the paths.

You don't have to know exactly what the different pathways are. You just have to be open to the possibilities that these different paths exist and that each one is safe and good.

There are so very many ways for the things that are right for you to become part of your life. From now on, know that you are at the center of all the paths, with the things that are right for you coming toward you in many wonderful ways—ways you may have never even imagined.

CLEANSING TO PAVE THE WAY

As we go through life, we pick up other people's energies, and thoughts that don't serve us. We also carry our own old ideas and beliefs that don't fit who we are right now. So it's important to know how to cleanse our personal energy fields and fill ourselves with pure life-force energy.

Begin by opening your heart to the presence of two Unicorn Guardians, one on either side of you. Take a few moments to connect to the energy of each Unicorn.

Now, with the Unicorns at your side, feel a shower of sparkling light energy beginning to flow down onto and into your body. This sparkling energy is perfectly attuned to who you're meant to be. Allow it to flow into your head, into your shoulders, and down your spine.

Take a moment to connect with this sparkling light energy as it flows through every part of your body. Feel it cleansing, purifying, and bringing you into a state of balance and wholeness.

As this sparkling light energy flows through you, feel it releasing and dissolving unwanted energy, old beliefs, and anything that doesn't align with your unique, authentic self.

Now do an internal scan. Use your intuition to sense if there's any particular spot within your body where the energy doesn't feel quite right. You might imagine it as a dark spot in your sparkling energy field.

Feel yourself at one with the Unicorns on either side of you, and feel their energy repairing and uplifting the grid that holds the structure of energy within and around you.

Feel any dark spots in your energy field disappear within the sacred trinity you form with the two beautiful beings at your side.

Feel old, stuck energy dissolving and disappearing, along with any energy that doesn't belong to you. Feel powerful, sparkling light energy take the place of limiting beliefs, self-doubts, and anything that's been holding you back from being your best, most expanded self.

Now stop for a moment, and get a sense of yourself in this beautiful, clean, pure state.

Ground yourself down into the loving energy of the Earth, and feel yourself centered, balanced, and radiant. Give your love to your Unicorn Guardians, and thank them for their continued presence.

See the day before you stretched out like a beautiful landscape, glittering with wonderful new ideas, inspirations, and opportunities. Know that you are an important part of this landscape, and that you bring to this day a wealth of possibilities through your own shining presence.

INVITE IN A GUARDIAN BEING

As you continue to open new possibilities, let's take a moment to look at the reason we tend to be open to so few possibilities. Why do we focus on such a limited view of what's possible?

Because it feels safe!

Needing to feel safe is a huge drive for all of us, whether we're aware of it or not.

In order to truly open to new possibilities, you need to feel that it's safe, and now is the perfect time to invite in a Guardian Being to support you on your journey to new potentials.

Start by taking in a nice fresh breath, bringing yourself back to the clear, sparkling state you experienced with the Unicorns at your sides. Connect with Angels in the four corners of the room or space you're in, and allow yourself to feel safe and uplifted by their presence.

Remember all the paths leading toward you, symbolizing so many ways your good can come into your life, and as you do, see or sense a Guardian Being appear before you.

If you don't get an immediate sense of a Guardian, then join with me in welcoming another Unicorn to be your Guardian in welcoming new possibilities. Sense this Unicorn or other Guardian before you, and open to receive its energy and wisdom.

Think of the possibilities you've experienced up to now in your life, and ask your Guardian to help you open to all the possibilities that are for your highest good right now.

Set an intention that you will become aware of more and more opportunities and new experiences that are right for you, and ask your Unicorn Guardian to support you.

Keep this Guardian in your awareness. Whenever you get a chance, remind yourself of its presence, and connect with its uplifting energy. Remember your intention to attract only the opportunities that are truly right for you. Know that your Guardian is at your side, joining with you to create expansion in beautiful, safe ways.

THE ENERGY OF POSSIBILITIES

Now let's make friends with the actual energy of new possibilities.

To begin, take a nice deep breath. As you exhale, ground yourself down into the Earth's embrace. Feel yourself centered, balanced, and fully in your body.

In your mind's eye, see a tiny bright spark appear in the air before you, and watch as it begins to sparkle and radiate a shimmering light. This is the energy of new possibilities, and as you watch it, it expands to fill the room or space around you. Feel yourself energized and awakened by this bright spark, and as you do, check in and notice what you feel in your body.

Continue to notice how you feel as you connect to this energy. Do you feel safe? If so, then thank this energy for its presence, and continue creating an ongoing relationship with it. If you don't feel safe, then call on the Guardian Being you invited forth previously, and ask it to serve as a bridge, creating a sacred space for you to get to know the energy of new possibilities in a way that feels safe.

Anchor in the positive feelings you experience within this energy field of new possibilities, and if it feels right, set an intention to carry this energy with you on an ongoing basis. As you carry this energy, you bring it into every situation you encounter, becoming an agent of positive change and expansion everywhere you go.

CREATE A SPACE IN YOUR HEART

So far, we've been opening ourselves to new possibilities and new potentials in order to more easily connect with and attract the things that are right for us. Now, with the help of your Unicorn Guardians, we'll create a space in your heart in which to welcome new possibilities.

New possibilities involve change of some kind, so check in with your attitudes toward change today. If there are places in your life that make you feel stuck, it may seem that the people or situations involved will never change. But in my lifetime, I've seen people and situations change (for the better) in ways I *never* could have expected!

Focus on your heart right now, and create a warm space there for new possibilities—possibilities that will bring lasting, positive change. Feel the supportive energy of your Unicorn Guardians at your sides, and feel the balancing and centering effect of this new space in your heart.

Breathe into the warmth of this space, and feel the energy of new possibilities expanding within you, spreading out all around you, and supporting you in being who you are truly meant to be.

As you go through your day, remind yourself of this space in your heart, and allow it to uplift you and empower you. Feel yourself at one with the energy of new possibilities!

A NEW GARDEN OF POSSIBILITIES

Now that you've created a place in your heart dedicated to new possibilities, it's time to create an inner experience of expansion.

Go within now and fill yourself with the beautiful, sparkling light energy we worked with earlier in this chapter. With every breath you take, bring in more and more of that beautiful sparkling energy until it completely fills your being.

Now get a sense of yourself in this beautiful, clean, pure state. As you do, imagine you are in a garden: a small, beautiful garden with high stone walls all around it. As you imagine yourself in this garden, look around and notice what you see growing here.

Now see yourself walking around and exploring. Walk along each of the four walls that make up your garden, taking in what you see.

The garden within these walls represents the possibilities you're currently allowing yourself to experience. Whatever you see within these four walls (your personal garden of possibilities) represents the potential you are currently allowing.

But you could have so much more!

Look around your garden again, and see the four walls begin to dissolve. See them becoming more and more invisible, until there are no more walls surrounding your garden. Now, as you look around, you see a beautiful landscape—a vast garden of possibilities, spread out in every direction as far as the eye can see.

See it as beautiful, vibrant, and alive, filled with every color, and vibrating with beautiful, positive life-force energy. The longer you stand and look around you in every direction, the more things you notice—so many more things than you had within the walls of your small garden.

Allow yourself to venture out now and walk through all the beautiful sights you see outside the old walls. Just choose one direction and walk, knowing that at any moment, you can choose a new direction.

You are free to try out all of these possibilities. You're free to see if you like them, and you're free to choose new possibilities that you think you might like. And as you do, this unlimited garden continues to grow, so that more and more possibilities are created, expanding the boundaries of your own existence, and expanding what is possible for you—and for everyone else.

Stand in this place and feel that expansion within you. Stand in this unlimited garden of possibilities and feel yourself connected to the life of the Earth beneath you and to the life all around you.

Know that this sense of connection will help you integrate the new possibilities and positive expansion you are experiencing. Feel yourself in this grounded space, and allow yourself to embrace all the positive possibilities without needing to know what they are right now.

Take in a deep breath as you look around at this beautiful space of possibilities and know that you can come back here in your mind as often as you like, breathing in new possibilities and expanding your inner self.

Know that as you expand your being to allow them, new possibilities will come to you one by one. Each new possibility will unfold itself in a beautiful way, and as it does, your life will continue to become more and more beautiful, more and more a reflection of who you are and what you love.

CHAPTER 8

꧁

GIVE YOURSELF PERMISSION

What have you accomplished in your life so far? It might be having kids, getting married, buying a home, or success in your career, if you have one. Or maybe you've attained a certain level of achievement in a sport or hobby.

The list of possibilities is endless, but let a few of the most important things come into your mind.

Think of these things in the form of a list. We'll call it List #1.

Now, think of the things you *want* to do or be or have—things you've been wanting for some time, but haven't experienced yet—and create a second list in your mind. These are your hopes and dreams and visions, the next step up in your life.

We could title List #1, "Things I have permission to do." We could title the second list, "Things I am *waiting for permission* to do."

Take a few moments to absorb this idea.

Think of everything you already have—the physical things you have, the intangible things you have, and the things you are—as things you feel you have *permission* to be or have.

Conversely, consider the dreams you've *not* experienced (the things you've been trying to create, without success) as things that haven't happened because you are still waiting to get *outside* permission.

It's a powerful thought, isn't it? Giving ourselves permission is vital if we're going to share *all* our gifts, but it's not always easy, because giving ourselves permission isn't something we've been given permission to do!

So to start, just open yourself to the awareness of your two lists. This awareness alone will begin a process of transformation that will unfold in a beautiful way.

WAITING FOR PERMISSION

Take a moment to think about what your family has given you permission to do and be and have in your life. (Most of the time the unspoken permission given is to do the things they've done!)

Our family creates a foundation for the things we feel we have permission to do, then as we grow up, we begin to go through cycles of achievement in school and work. If we receive approval for our performance, we're given permission to advance to the next level of achievement.

When we're growing up, the permission to go to the next level always comes from someone outside us. Having that outside permission makes us feel that we're allowed to do something, that we're good enough to do that thing, and most importantly, *that doing it is safe.*

This need to be safe is so powerful that it often keeps us from living our dreams. Without realizing it, we wait and wait for permission in the form of outside approval or opportunity.

This can show up as waiting to be discovered if you're in a creative field or waiting to be noticed in any form—waiting for someone else to give you permission so that you can feel safe.

Ask yourself: "What do I fear might happen if I gave myself permission to be and have the things I dream of?" Take this question seriously and look deep inside yourself for the answer.

Then ask: Who do I feel is the ultimate permission-giver in my life? This might be a parent or some other authority figure. (For me, it's always been my dad.) Stick with the question until you have a strong sense of the answer.

Now think of three major things you've accomplished. Who gave you permission to do them?

Think of the things you want to do or be or have. Who specifically do you need permission from in order to experience these things?

Allow your personal energy to expand as you continue to contemplate these questions, and feel your heart becoming more and more empowered and free.

CLEANSING AND AWAKENING

The more we free ourselves from needing outside permission, the more our heart expands, the more grounded we become, and the more powerful we are.

But tuning in to the need for permission can be painful, so let's turn to cleansing all the places inside us where lack of permission has caused us pain.

Take in a nice deep breath, and as you release it, relax and imagine that you're standing in a warm, healing waterfall. Facing you on either side are your Guardian Unicorns.

The water flowing from above is gentle and soothing, and as it flows it reaches all the places in your being that have felt not good enough or embarrassed or afraid. These old feelings are gently unstuck and washed away now, leaving your powerful, pure, unique energy intact.

Your Guardian Unicorns envelop you in their sparkling energy, and your personal energy grid is strengthened and upgraded as you stand between them. Spend a few moments experiencing the wonder of your upgraded energy system, then shine love from your heart down to the center of the loving Earth.

When you're ready, step out of the waterfall and walk with your Unicorn Guardians to a nearby natural pool of water. This is a pool of awakening, and as you step down into it, you feel every part of you waking up.

The longer you stay in this pool, the more energized and awakened you feel.

When you are ready, step out of the pool into the warmth of the Sun. Ground yourself once more into the love of the Earth. Say thank you to the Earth, the Sun, and your Guardian Unicorns as you feel the golden rays of the Sun empowering you to expand into everything you want to be.

Take these golden rays with you, and know that I am seeing you shining!

THE KIND OF SAFETY YOU TRULY NEED

Although we all have to put some kind of energy into everything that we create, some things definitely come easier than others. Some things almost feel like paint by numbers; we just do them, without internal struggle.

Those are the things we've been given permission to do. For some of us, getting married and having kids is not a big struggle because that's what our parents did, and so we have permission to do it as well.

With that as an example, start getting a clearer picture of your own set of internal permissions. Then start setting yourself free. One way to begin is by looking at this question: What does it *really mean* to give yourself permission?

I think it has to do with making a deep decision not to reject yourself, no matter what happens, and to view life as an adventure rather than a test.

When you allow yourself to view life as a process of trial and error, you become energetically bigger and stronger with each situation you experience.

At its core, waiting for permission has to do with two things: needing to be good enough and needing to feel safe. We wait for an outside seal of approval before we allow ourselves to reach for—or succeed at—something new, because we don't feel safe without that approval.

This awareness alone helps us begin to break free from the needing-permission cycle, because, if you really think about it, having permission has *not* kept you safe!

The kind of safety you *truly* need is something you access from deep within yourself: the knowledge that you'll stay true to yourself, that you won't give up on yourself no matter what, that you'll forgive yourself when necessary, that you'll keep moving toward your dreams, and that you'll never abandon yourself.

Also deep inside you is the knowledge that you are not alone and that connecting to your Guardians will help you return to a feeling of safety and rightness.

Begin now to treat each day as a grand adventure, and see yourself as not only brave, but *resilient*.

YOUR PLACE AT THE TABLE

As you become more comfortable giving yourself permission, it's important to tune in to your body and connect to the love and support of the Earth.

Think of something you want to do that you haven't been given permission to do, and as you think about it, notice what you feel in your body. You might feel a sense of tightness or heaviness in a certain part of your body; if so, just relax and breathe into that part of yourself.

Feel the presence of your Guardian Dragon and step into its energy field. Soak in the love and powerful support of this energy, and take a few moments to receive any insights or messages your Guardian Dragon has for you.

Send energetic roots deep down into the Earth, and feel the energy of the Earth welcome you. Draw love and nourishment up through your roots, and let this love and nourishment fill your body. Take another moment to check in and notice what you feel in your body.

Now, as we did in Chapter 5, imagine life itself as a banquet. In your mind's eye, see a beautiful banquet table stretching out in both directions farther than the eye can see, and see before you your place at the table. See a place card with your name on it, and allow yourself to take your rightful place there.

Seated at this table, you see again that it's not just a place to receive the Earth's bounty, but also a place to share your own gifts.

Your place at the table can only be filled by you, and it is best filled when you are fully connected to your heart and your true heart's desires.

Only you can create and give to the world from this place, so take a deep breath now, and send that breath to your solar plexus. Feed your solar plexus loving permission energy as you think of something you want to do or be or have.

Say to yourself, "I choose, and as I do, I bless the world. I have a place at the table of life, and the world is waiting for me to share my gifts."

Commune with your Guardian Dragon once more before you step out of its energy.

Hold your place at the table within your heart, and know that I am thanking you for the gift you are.

PERMISSION GRANTED

Are you feeling more in tune with and connected to the energy of permission? The more aligned we are with this energy, the freer we are to follow our inner guidance and fulfill our life purpose.

Relax, and let a wonderful sense of safety fill your body, mind, and spirit. Allow yourself to go to a place of wisdom deep within you, and see yourself in a beautiful hallway with office doors on either side of you. See yourself standing in front of an old-fashioned office door, and notice that the writing on the door says, "Office of Permissions for (your name)."

As you enter the room, you see that you are inside a large old-fashioned office, and as you look around, you see a massive desk with a chair in front of it. Behind the desk sits a large, distinguished-looking older man. In front of him on the desk is a large solid-gold stamp that reads: Permission Granted, Success Guaranteed.

The man invites you to take a seat in front of his desk, and as you do, you realize that you are holding a folder. When you open the folder, you see it's filled with pages in your own handwriting, and each page is requesting permission for something you want to do or be or have.

As you flip through the pages and read their words, you realize that the pages represent who you are and what you love. They represent your natural expansion, but you don't know if it's safe to ask for so much, so you hand the folder to the man behind the desk.

As you do, you notice he is wearing a beautiful gold lapel pin, with writing on it that you can't quite make out.

The man looks at the pages in your folder, and then he looks up at you. He studies you for a long time. As he studies you, the man smiles and then begins to become more and more transparent.

As he begins to fade, you feel yourself become centered and more grounded. You feel your body, mind, and spirit become integrated, and you feel a powerful surge of your own life-force energy.

You watch him slowly disappear, and as he does you feel stronger, more alive, and happier than you've ever felt.

Finally, he is completely gone, and you stand and walk around the desk to his chair. On the seat of the chair is a lapel pin that reads, "There is no worthiness; there is only choice."

You attach this pin to your own clothing, and sit down in the chair. Now you open your folder again.

Look at each page separately now, and read what it is that you want to be and do and have.

Pick up the "Permission Granted, Success Guaranteed" stamp. With a feeling of safety and joy, see yourself using that heavy gold stamp to press "Permission Granted, Success Guaranteed" on every page.

When you are ready, come back into full waking consciousness, carrying your wisdom within you and feeling a difference within yourself.

Feel the truth of your new knowledge within your own heart: there is no worthiness; there is only choice.

Say thank you to the Earth and the energy of permission. You carry this beautiful energy within you now.

Go through the days to come feeling mentored by the Universe, creating the things that make your heart sing. Know you are supported, know you are loved, and know you are safe.

❦

CHAPTER 9

TRUST YOURSELF

You are meant to create a life that reflects your own unique inner truth.

But as we go through life, it seems like we all get less and less in touch with our own truths, and more in touch with *other* people's truths. And the more we get out of touch with what's right for us, the more disconnected from our own authentic selves we become.

Most of us have been taught, in hundreds of subtle ways, *not* to trust ourselves. We're taught that it's selfish or even dangerous. We're taught to ignore our own inner voice and to trust in the judgment of the people around us instead. This takes us so far out of alignment with our own truth that it's easy to find ourselves feeling overwhelmed and drained.

We begin a habit of reacting to life—just coping—without knowing how to proactively create a life that's right for us.

I believe your own inner voice is meant to guide you in *all* things, and I also believe that every decision you make in opposition to your own inner wisdom is destined to fail in one way or another.

Trusting yourself is never selfish. It's wise.

In this chapter we'll journey together to deeper, more grounded self-trust, and the first step is to start thinking of your life as a work in progress, rather than something you should have *already* perfected. Together, we'll build on the work of the previous chapters and give ourselves permission to live by trial and error.

How would it feel to view your life as one big science experiment, within which you get to see, through trial and error, what you can create and what feels best for you? Consider this as you open yourself to greater self-trust, safe in the knowledge that your inner wisdom will guide you truly and help you make adjustments when necessary.

RECOGNIZE YOUR OWN POWER

Viewing life as your own personal science experiment can best be accomplished by becoming conscious of the choices you are making *and* the outcomes you are experiencing as a result of those choices.

Living this way will deepen your self-trust and connect you to your power to choose.

No matter what it feels like at times, no one can take away your power. It can only be given away. In fact, we *trade* away our power in exchange for the things we need: affection, security, approval, you name it!

The trouble is, when you give away your power in a relationship, it causes an imbalance at the relationship's core. This unbalanced power dynamic weakens the relationship, damaging it more and more as time goes by.

In order to get to a healthy place of empowerment, view yourself with compassion and begin to understand your reasons for making the choices you've made in the past.

I believe you've had valid reasons for every choice you've made. Your choices may not have been conscious or they may have been made out of fear, but on some level, they made sense. (We'll talk more about this in Chapter 15.)

In every moment, no matter what situation you find yourself in, you have the power to choose.

For example, let's imagine a woman we'll call Mary. Mary is in her 60s, has been married 40 years, and is unhappy with her marriage. She feels guilty for feeling lonely and unfulfilled, so she blames herself for her feelings and tries to silence her inner voice. She feels increasingly powerless to be happy in her marriage and her life.

She goes around and around in a circle, trying to change her husband in order to get her emotional needs met. When she hits bottom with that, she swings the opposite way and blames herself for feeling the way she feels, thinking she should just be happy with what she has. She continues to bounce back and forth between these two states, experiencing less energy and more illness as time goes on.

But if Mary is willing to recognize her own power to choose, she'll be able to see the situation with new clarity. She'll see that changing her husband isn't a real option, and neither is changing the truth of how she feels.

She'll realize that she is using her power to choose by choosing to stay in her marriage. She *could* choose to leave her home, face the unknown, and start a new life. But the truth is, she would rather stay with her husband and continue living the life she knows. She recognizes that she's actually willing to stay in a less-than-fulfilling relationship in order to keep the family home together for her children and grandchildren to visit. She's just not comfortable with the thought of major change.

Once she sees her power and recognizes that it's *her* choice, she reclaims her empowerment. She clearly sees that she's choosing to give up one thing in order to have another.

She also understands that she has the power to make a new choice at any time. This will carry her forward into positive change, even if she continues to choose to stay in her marriage.

Life is set up to support you in living the life that's right for you, and you can trust your inner wisdom to guide you to a life that gets better and better. Options always exist, but they remain unseen until you listen to your inner voice and connect to your Greater Self.

You are never as trapped as you think.

Your own inner wisdom is in sync with a universal force for good. When you follow your inner guidance—when you trust yourself—you step into the flow of that good.

THE LIGHT OF YOUR AWARENESS

The subject of self-trust has deep roots. Most of us have a few ongoing issues that have been around a long time. We may even have given up on resolving those chronic issues because everything we've tried in the past has failed and the only solutions we're aware of sound worse than the problems themselves! We feel helpless to change.

So we take these "unresolvable" issues and shove them behind us, out of view. It's as if we have toxic material that we don't know what to do with, so we stuff it in a trash bag and drag it around behind us, where we don't have to look at it. We try to pretend it's not there, but its toxicity leaks into everything we do.

In order to bring ourselves back into balance, we need to bring all our issues into the light of our awareness now. What this means in practical terms is that you become completely honest with yourself about how you feel about everything in your life.

One of the first things that happens when we stop trusting ourselves is we stop being honest with ourselves about how we feel. We don't validate how we feel, and we certainly don't view our feelings as a reliable guiding force.

We numb ourselves to how we feel, and as we do, we numb ourselves to the guidance that will bring solutions.

Imagine you are standing within a pillar of light, surrounded by the energy of your Guardian Angel. In front of you is an ancient Tree stump with a large flat surface. You feel supported by the good will coming from the spirit of this old, old Tree, and you feel empowered and energized by the presence of your Guardian Angel.

Bring your attention now to the pillar of light shining down upon you, and bring one of your issues into this light. See a three-dimensional representation of your issue take form on top of the Tree stump before you.

Take a deep breath, let it out slowly, and in this powerful light, allow yourself to see your issue fully. See it for what it is, and identify your true feelings about this matter.

Do you feel anything in your body as you do this? If so, gently say, "I love you," to this part of your body, and breathe light into it.

Try not to get overwhelmed by your feelings. Just let them come into the light of your awareness, and accept that they are there. You may discover several different feelings; if so, try to focus on the most meaningful.

If possible, distill it to a single word, and complete this sentence: When it comes to this situation, I feel _____.

*Bring this sentence with you back into your normal awareness,
and see it filled with light. Don't worry about doing anything about
this newly clarified feeling. Bringing—and keeping—it in the light of
your awareness will begin a process of change from within.*

From now on, be willing to be honest with yourself about how
you feel about everything that's going on in your life. This is easier
said than done, I know! But stick with me here.

The main things that keep us from this willingness are: (a) the
fact that we don't know how to change things, and (b) we're afraid
of what we *think* we'd have to do in order to change things.

For example, if we're unhappy in a job, we may think the only
solution is to quit, and since we're afraid that quitting would leave
us worse off, we stuff our unhappy feeling behind us.

But if you can be courageous enough to bring your feelings out,
place them into the light, and keep them there—just being honest
with yourself every day about how you feel, without thinking you
need to have an answer—you'll get back in sync with your inner
wisdom, and with the universal force for good that surrounds you.
Positive change will begin to happen organically.

Be gentle with yourself, and remember that trusting yourself
and being honest with yourself go hand in hand.

YOUR OWN TRUE PATH

No matter how challenging life is, if you can be *honest* with
yourself, you'll get back in alignment with your authentic self. Once
you are in alignment with that authentic self, you're back on the
path that's right for you.

When you follow other people's guidance in place of your own,
you step off your true path, and the minute you do that, you find
yourself lost—in an unfamiliar, scary neighborhood where all the
streetlights are broken.

The more you listen to others instead of yourself, the more lost
you become, and the harder it is to find your way back to your true
path. Of course, it's never too late to return to your true path. But it's
better to stay on it in the first place by following your *own* guidance.

Sometimes your own true path can *also* seem scary, but there are lampposts to light your way—and when you are on your own path, you'll always be moving forward instead of going in circles.

When you bring your issues into the light of your own awareness by being honest about how you feel, you step back on your own true path, and from there, in time, you'll see the next step. If you can stay honest about how you feel without feeling that you need to come up with a solution, a solution will present itself to you.

It may not be a complete solution. It may just be the next step: something small and doable—something you'll feel right about. Taking action with this small step in the right direction will empower you and put you in touch with more of your life force, making you feel awakened and energized.

As you know, we tend to have a very narrow focus when it comes to seeing possible solutions to our problems. Once you begin being honest with yourself about your issues, the solutions you need will come to you in small increments—bit by bit—without your having to struggle to think them up yourself.

Let me remind you: there are many, many possible solutions to whatever problems you face. I promise you they exist! You may not be able to see them yet, but the more you get back into alignment with your authentic self, the more they'll become visible to you.

One by one and step by step, answers, solutions, ideas, and new situations will come to you, and your life will begin to unfold in a brand-new way. The simple act of connecting to your truth puts you into a state of flow within which you are magnetic to answers, solutions, and the forward movement that will take you to where you really want to be.

FEEL YOURSELF FULLY IN YOUR BODY

The next step on your path to self-trust is to get fully in touch with your body and begin honoring it as a powerful guidance system. Most of us spend too much time in our heads and not centered within our physical forms. We project our energy outside of us, focusing on how we appear to others, worrying about what others think, and contemplating the future.

But our inner wisdom often speaks to us in a physical way, so it's important for us to be centered and grounded in our physical bodies.

Take a moment right now to feel yourself fully in your body. Where do you feel the energy the most? Make it a practice to stop what you're doing a few times a day and focus your awareness on the energy in the different parts of your body.

Once, when I'd had a really stressful day, I checked in with my body and got the feeling that my root chakra at the base of my spine needed extra support. In my stressed-out state, I didn't feel very connected to my Guardians, so I closed my eyes and sent out a kind of "distress call," asking for a Guardian to help support me.

Immediately I felt the presence of a giant Redwood Tree envelop me, and as I soaked in its presence, I realized it was a giant Sequoia. I felt like I was inside this beautiful Tree Being, with its roots helping connect me both to the Earth and to the other Redwoods.

Open your heart now to call to the Spirit of the Redwood Trees. Feel a giant Redwood Tree answer your call, and feel yourself inside the energy of this beautiful being.

Within the loving, supportive energy of this giant Tree, you feel grounded, supported by the Earth, and surrounded by the love of all the other Trees.

Within this love, focus on and feel the energy in your feet . . . in your calves and shins . . . in your knees . . . your thighs . . . your pelvis . . . your abdomen . . . your back . . . your chest . . . your shoulders . . . your arms . . . your hands . . . your neck . . . your jaw . . . and your head.

Take the time to really feel the energy in each part of your body.

Thank the Trees with love as you open your eyes and look around you now, still feeling alive in every part of your body.

From now on, take a few moments each morning to connect with the Redwoods and feel yourself fully in your body. This ongoing practice will support you in connecting with your inner wisdom and trusting the guidance that comes forth.

One of the places where people commonly feel body guidance is in their abdominal area, so start paying attention to how your stomach feels as you interact with others. Before I began to do this work, I used to experience a reaction in my stomach whenever I talked with a certain friend. I couldn't understand why I felt this way, because she was always saying positive, polite things. I ended up blaming myself for the lousy way I felt whenever I was around her.

What I came to know is this: I can trust my stomach! It turned out my friend had quite a bit of negativity (some of it toward me) that she wasn't verbally expressing.

When someone is using nice words, but what they are saying doesn't match up with what they're *really* thinking and feeling, I feel that discrepancy in my stomach. I'm willing to bet that you will too, once you bring your consciousness back into your body.

I've learned the hard way to trust my gut, to trust my own instincts, and to trust how my body feels in any given moment. In my work with clients over the years, I've observed that people's bodies are always giving them very accurate signals, but these signals are often ignored.

In some cases, people report that they don't have any feelings at all in certain areas of their bodies. If this is the case with you, set an intention to regain awareness of your body at a pace that's gentle and safe, and for your highest good. Use this intention as a sort of safety net, and be patient with yourself as you regain body awareness.

Begin a practice of getting fully back in your body, trusting what you feel there.

BECOME THE CREATOR OF SOMETHING BEAUTIFUL

It's easy to get wrapped up in the events of life and find yourself living in reactive mode. But in order to live a life that fully expresses who you are and what you love, you need to live proactively.

Begin to think of yourself as a creator, one who is creating something beautiful. That beautiful creation is your life. No matter how "unbeautiful" your life may seem right now, the more you trust yourself and give yourself permission to choose, the more beautiful and satisfying it will become.

Once you get in touch with your true feelings and open yourself to allow new solutions, you can begin to make choices. When you get clear in your own heart and mind about what you want to create, and when you *trust* those choices, your choices will start to become magnetic. They'll take on a life of their own in order to manifest in the best way. But you have to give yourself permission to choose first.

Don't be hampered by what's "realistic." Don't think you have to figure out how to make it happen. Just consciously choose what you would love to create, and *keep* choosing it, within your mind and your heart. Connect to Source love as you do this, and remember: trusting yourself makes you both strong and wise.

BE PATIENT WITH YOURSELF

As you begin to embody the energy of self-trust, remember that it's best not to attempt wholesale, radical change.

Pay attention to your own comfort level; you can only move as fast as the slowest part of you can move. I'm going to say that again because I think it's so important: *you can only move as fast as the slowest part of you can move.*

That "slowest part" may be the part of you that's afraid, a part that craves security above all else. That part of you can be very strong, so you'll actually grow more quickly if you *don't* try to push yourself faster than your own willingness to change.

When we force ourselves to make changes we're not ready for, the changes we make don't last. You *will* need to move beyond your comfort zone, but give yourself permission to do it gently. Put your focus on connecting to the truth inside you, and let it guide you in small, incremental steps, according to what feels right.

Returning to a state of self-trust doesn't have to be scary, abrupt, or radical. Simply move into alignment with your Greater Self bit by bit, and you will begin to attract to you everything you need to live according to your life purpose.

Remember, our guidance comes to us in the form of positive energy toward what we would love to be, do, and have. Love is what powers the Universe. Everything else just falls away—unless you give it life through your own energy.

Your power lies in getting in touch with your own inner truth, getting back in alignment with your inner guidance, and focusing on what you love. Love has its own magnetic power and will grow and grow, attracting to you and creating for you everything that's right for you.

That's what you are meant to have, and it's also what the world *needs* for you to have. The world needs you to create a life that is the perfect expression of your beauty and your truth.

CHAPTER 10

∽⚬∽

REINVENT YOURSELF

Reinventing yourself is actually just a process of becoming more of who you really are. It doesn't have to be a big, scary, total reinvention. You can reinvent just a part of yourself, if you choose. This keeps you evolving, and more and more in tune with who you're meant to be.

For many years I used an image of a swan in my business logo as a reminder of the Hans Christian Andersen story, "The Ugly Duckling." In the story, the hero struggles time after time to fulfill himself as a duck, always meeting with failure and frustration. It's only when he sees what he really is (a beautiful swan) that he truly begins to live his life.

In the same way, lasting fulfillment only comes to each one of us when we align with the part of us that knows who and what we truly are.

The goal is to become more aware of, and in alignment with, your Greater Self, because the more connected you are to your Greater Self, the more you're able to manifest your own authentic, original inner blueprint and live the life that's right for you.

As you become more and more consciously connected to your Greater Self, you'll naturally find yourself engaging in the activities that use your gifts and talents to the fullest, because your Greater Self holds the energy pattern for what will make you happiest and most fulfilled.

And this is an important point: rather than giving you a list of preset ideas that helps you make choices, your connection to your Greater Self enables you to receive moment-by-moment guidance.

The better aligned you are with your Greater Self, the more Source energy flows through your original inner blueprint, and the more fulfilled you feel.

In this chapter we'll be journeying together through the process of reinvention, bit by bit becoming more of who you truly are.

TAKE STOCK

An important step in the reinvention process is to take stock of where you are out of alignment with your Greater Self. This is easy to do, because the places you're out of alignment with your Greater Self are the places in your life where you don't feel fulfilled.

It might be a relationship that doesn't feel right, a job that doesn't feel good, and so on. As we move through this chapter, open your mind to become aware of the parts of your life that don't feel the way you want them to feel.

Relax as you do this. You don't have to figure out a way to *solve* your problems. Just notice what they are. As always, awareness begins a process of transforming issues from the inside out.

As you go through the day, periodically stop and do an "internal scan" of your work, your relationships, your body, your activities, and so forth. Allow yourself to become fully conscious of the places in your life that don't feel good. These are all connected to parts of yourself that you can now choose to reinvent.

Have you heard the old rocket-ship analogy? Imagine launching a rocket ship aimed at the moon. You might have the rocket aimed perfectly when you launch it, but because the moon is so far away from the launch pad, even minor shifts in the trajectory of the ship will cause it to go way off course. Over time, you'll end up in a very different place from where you had intended.

This analogy describes the small changes—tiny little shifts and adjustments we may not even be conscious of making—that result in a feeling of being off course and unfulfilled. We make these course adjustments because we feel we should or because it's what someone else wants or because we've been taught it's the right thing to do.

Or maybe we just don't have enough confidence in ourselves to truly follow our hearts.

We trade away what feels good for what feels safe or what we think we *have* to do. But when you ignore the inner guidance that comes in the form of a not-good feeling, you alter the course of your own trajectory and take yourself off course. Over time, you may even end up moving in the *opposite* direction of your Greater Self's intended destination.

The further off course you become—the more you travel in the wrong direction—the less access you have to your own life force. When this happens, everything you do seems harder, and living takes a lot more effort.

Taking stock of which parts of your life don't feel good puts you back in touch with your own guidance system and turns you back in the right direction.

Once you're traveling in the right direction, you'll feel a rush of energy, because you'll be in better alignment with your Greater Self, with greater access to the flow of your own life force.

Remember, you don't have to figure out any of this. It's already encoded within you. Your Greater Self already knows everything you need to know—you just have to get more in alignment with that Greater Self.

ASSESS THE ROLES YOU'VE ACCEPTED

As we take advantage of opportunities to reinvent ourselves, it's important to look at the roles we've accepted. Roles consist of *preformed* ideas of how we should act in certain situations. The roles we take on play a big part in which paths we travel in life—and where we eventually end up.

The end result of assuming a role can be very different from what we expect.

We often assume roles such as Wife, Daughter, Mother, Daughter-in-Law, Mother-in-Law, Friend, Teacher, and Healer. It's not the function itself that's unhealthy—of course we might choose to experience being a wife, parent, and so on. The trouble sets in when we act from the *role* and not from our authentic choices.

When you lock yourself into a role, you are acting according to outside programming, instead of listening to your own inner guidance.

Take a deep breath now, feel the presence of your Guardian Dragon standing with you, and go within to take a look at the roles you currently occupy. Are there any places in your life where you feel trapped or constricted by a role? Just gently observe yourself.

It's not necessary for you to immediately make radical, life-changing decisions concerning the roles you've been playing, but it *is* important to become aware of the fact that roles, by their very nature, become stale with time.

The minute you lock yourself into a role, it begins to decay. Energy likes to be in a state of flow, and your life force flows best when you are present in each moment, tapped into your own internal guidance. When you lock yourself into a predetermined role, your actions are then based on the role, instead of what feels right for you. Over time, the role becomes more and more stale and lifeless.

The word *should* can act as an alarm signal, letting you know when you are living from a role instead of your authentic self. When you catch yourself thinking, "As a (insert role here), I should (insert thing that's *not* aligned with your heart's desire here)."

For example I might think, "As a Mother, I should automatically say yes to the family event my grown child is asking me to hold, because that's what a Good Mother would do." But by automatically acting from the *role* of Mother, I've bypassed the inner guidance that is so vital to living my life purpose.

Instead, upon receiving the request, I can take a minute to check in with myself and see if I truly *want* to hold such an event. If my own internal energy is pointing me toward doing it—if I get an energized feeling when I think of it—then I'll be acting from my inner guidance, and holding the event will be something that helps me live out my soul purpose *and* serves the world.

If I know right away that I *don't* really want to hold the event, I have two very different choices before me. I can act from the role of Good Mother, push my authentic feelings down, and say yes. But because I'm taking an action that's out of alignment with my inner guidance, I'll be altering my true trajectory and taking myself off course (both in my life and in my relationship with my child).

No rule book (or role book!) can tell us, in advance, the right thing to do in every situation. Only your inner guidance can be completely trusted, because your inner guidance is connected to the Greater Self that has the wisdom and "big picture" knowledge the rule books lack.

If I take the second choice and tell my grown child that my guidance isn't supporting me in holding the event, he might be upset at first. But it will give us an opportunity to be completely honest with each other about how we really feel, and without this kind of honesty, our relationship will always be stunted.

Our roles program us to *always give*—but giving isn't always the best thing for us to do! When you follow the guidance of where your own energy is pointing, you can rest in the knowledge that your guidance is working on behalf of the highest good for *all*.

When a role calls for you to do something that your inner energy is pulling you away from, you might find that it's actually better for all involved if *someone else* ends up doing the task.

When you choose to experience yourself as a parent or teacher or friend, of course there will be hard or unpleasant tasks you'll have to perform. But when you put yourself in alignment with your Greater Self (by following your guidance), you'll find yourself either *wanting* to perform a task, or at the very least, finding yourself just naturally doing it and feeling good about it.

Many times we're afraid to bring our awareness to the parts of our lives that are out of alignment because of a desire to spare ourselves pain or guilt. But remember, you don't have to figure out how to change everything. Just be willing to look at your roles.

You now have the power to decide who you are going to be, according to your *own* wisdom. You can always choose to change in ways that are doable and manageable and feel positive!

The correct trajectory is already encoded within you, and the Universe is set up to support the manifestation of your life purpose.

Your intention to become more in alignment with your Greater Self, together with the willingness to look at where you are out of alignment, will begin a powerful process of transformation from within.

BE YOUR OWN MIRROR

Now let's turn our focus to learning to be your own mirror, which will mean that you, once and for all, stop asking for permission to be who you really are.

Being your own mirror means becoming the *only* judge of what's right for you. As we've seen, it's easy to get locked into roles and find ourselves living a life of conforming to other people's desires.

We conform because we're afraid *not* to conform. Many times we're motivated by a need to overcome disapproval from the past, stuck in an endless loop of trying to prove ourselves worthy. This need for approval, more than anything, keeps us trapped.

Over time it causes so many shifts in our trajectory that we may end up on a strange planet or even lost in the middle of space, with very little life force flowing through us. Daily life becomes drudgery, and we feel stuck, overwhelmed, and completely devoid of energy.

When you're disconnected from the choices and actions that make you who you are, you have less and less life force flowing through you. But the minute you find the courage to point yourself back toward what's true for you, you'll feel life flowing back into your being.

So hasten your own reinvention and stop asking for permission to be exactly who you are.

If you are feeling controlled by someone in your life, recognize that this person is not in alignment with his or her own Greater Self. We all need to give ourselves permission to be our true selves, and when you get back in touch with the choices that are right for you, you radiate an energy that uplifts everyone (whether the people around you recognize it or not). *If it is right for you, it is right.*

From now on, catch yourself when you are trying to prove yourself worthy, comparing yourself to someone else, or asking for validation. When you're engaged in these behaviors, it's a signal that you're cut off from your Greater Self, and thus feeling unsure of yourself.

Whenever you feel unsure of yourself, know that you are disconnected from your Greater Self—facing away from your own truth, not giving yourself permission to be who you are, and not valuing the unique beauty that is you.

Take a deep breath, ground yourself into the love of the Earth, and take a moment to make a mental list of the people you allow to be your mirrors.

Now, still feeling embraced by Earth energy, feel Source love flowing into and through you. Take another deep breath, let it out, and turn inward with the intention of connecting to your Greater Self.

Feel the beautiful energy of your Greater Self flowing into your heart, mind, body, and spirit. Feel yourself becoming energetically bigger in order to contain it.

Feel your own roots anchoring you into the love and support of the Earth as you bring more and more of your Greater Self into the physical world.

Now sit in communion with the wisdom of your Greater Self.

From this place of connection with Source, the Earth, and your Greater Self, give yourself permission to be your own mirror, reflecting back your own truth, courage, and beauty every single day.

BE PROACTIVE AS THE CREATOR OF YOUR LIFE

Life seems to be coming at us so fast, and it's easy to get stuck in reactive mode. But you are meant to be a creator, not a reactor.

I believe you're meant to create a life that expresses who you are and what you love, sharing your inner gifts with the world.

Begin to think of yourself as someone who is evolving, over the course of your lifetime, into a person who expresses more and more of your authentic self—creating beautiful things and experiences that express your essence.

In order to live this way, you need to become proactive. Instead of just reacting to life, get into the habit of deciding how *you* want things in your life to be. Life will bring to you the things that match the essence of whatever is activated within you, and your empowerment as the creator of your life is just waiting to be activated.

You can activate it bit by bit by choosing to act on what feels right to you in every moment as you focus on creating what *you* choose. This corrects your course, turning you more and more toward a life that feels better and better every day.

Create a morning practice of deciding how you want your day to unfold, picturing yourself having the experiences you choose and allowing yourself to experience the good feelings that come with the fulfillment of your wishes.

Today, I will remember that the Universe is supporting me as I create a life filled with _____ and _____.

Today, my intention is to surround myself with the energy of _____ and to feel _____ all day.

Specifically today, I see myself _____ and feeling _____ about it.

I feel love in my heart for life itself, and I am grateful for the Source love that flows through me and out into the world—in the form of the things I am, the things I do, and the things I have.

I am sometimes surprised by the words that come through me as I fill in the blanks—they can be different every day. Connect with Source energy through the love in your heart, and let it bring your choices to life.

LET THE PROCESS BE ORGANIC

Let your inner process of evolving and "becoming" be organic. Connecting to your Greater Self and living your unique life purpose is a process of awakening from within. You don't have to figure it out or force it.

Your job is simply to *support* it by connecting to your Greater Self. Your Greater Self knows every facet of your life purpose and can help you create an amazing life—the life you are meant to live. (I'm living proof, and if I can do it, so can you!)

By trusting your inner wisdom, you can reinvent yourself bit by bit, becoming a bigger version of yourself and expressing more of your life purpose every day.

Sometimes when we have an area of our lives that isn't working, we become very limited in our focus and in our idea of what is needed to change the situation. We often need to take a breath and open ourselves again to the wide world of possibilities. We need to remember that *no matter the problem we face, there are many solutions.*

Let this truth sink into your core and carry it with you from now on. *There is always a solution to whatever problem you face.* In fact, there are actually several solutions.

If you don't see a solution, it's only because you are still focusing on the problem. We tend to keep looking where the solution *isn't*, thinking, "It has to be there!"

If instead, you hold fast to the belief that a positive solution *does* exist, and you focus on *that*—not trying to figure out what the solution is, just knowing that it exists—you are aimed in the direction of the solution, and you will begin attracting it. You'll become magnetic to the solution, and your life can't help but transform at that point.

You now have tools you can use over and over to evolve into the bigger self that is just waiting to expand into a better life, a life that feels *right*—a life that inspires you every day and fills you with energy and optimism and power.

CHAPTER 11

꒰ ✿ ꒱

OPEN TO RECEIVE

Most of us are much more comfortable giving than receiving. In fact, I'm willing to bet that *you* actually give much more than you receive. So in this chapter we'll make friends with the energy of receiving—learning how to receive in a way that helps us connect to Source and align with a higher vibration.

I believe that everything you receive is really just an expression of the love the Universe has for you. In this chapter we'll focus on tapping into that truth, knowing it at a deep level, and opening yourself to receive more universal love in the form of experiences you have.

Let's jump right in with a practical shift you can experience right away.

> Go within and ask yourself, "How do I receive compliments? What am I really feeling as I say thank you?" Take a few minutes to get a clear sense of how it feels for you to receive.

> Now let's create a new receiving practice. The next time you receive something and say thank you (whether it's a compliment, a gift, or change at the grocery store), take a quick moment to tune in to your heart.

> Feel your energetic roots in the Earth connecting and welcoming you to the world, and at the same time feel Source love pouring into you from above, filling you with life. From this place of sacred balance, tune in to the energy of your heart, and say thank you.

Start practicing this right away by thinking about the last time you said thank you. Imagine you are within that experience again. Connect to the love of the Earth and feel your place at the table of life. Feel Source love pouring into you from above, and from that place of balance connect to your heart, and then say thank you.

This only takes a moment to do, and it will get easier and more natural with time.

RECEIVING AND YOUR BELIEFS

Does your spiritual belief system support you in receiving? Many of us have evolved and grown into spiritual beliefs that are different than the ones we were raised with. Look at your own beliefs, and see if they support you in not only giving, but receiving as well.

Most of the traditional religions we were raised with support us in being out-of-balance givers. We even have a saying: "It's better to give than to receive."

Look at this issue in your own life and see if you are out of balance as far as needing to *always* be the giver. Do you feel it's noble and good to give, but selfish to receive?

Even if you've adopted a spiritual belief system as an adult that supports you in receiving, there may still be old programming running inside you, under the surface.

So ask yourself now: "When you receive something, who do you believe you are really receiving from?"

If old programs are running, you may still believe that you have to be worthy in order to receive from a judging God. Or you may feel that opening to receive more than you already have is wrong.

Or do you believe there's a universal force that's supporting you in creating and expanding, and all you need to do is to get yourself in alignment with the love of this universal force in order to expand?

Look at your deep-down beliefs. Simply looking at them will begin to activate your own truth and help you get more in alignment with that truth. This will begin to shift the issue of receiving for you and transform not only how you think, but also how much you will be open to receive and hold in the future.

YOUR EXPERIENCE OF RECEIVING

As we focus on opening to receive, let's check in and look at what your experience of receiving has been in the past. Take a moment to reflect upon this and open yourself to a greater awareness of what's going on inside you when it comes to receiving.

One of the things that keeps us from being able to receive is the presence of hidden "price tags" that are sometimes attached to the things we're given.

Have you learned that sometimes it's better *not* to receive, because you'll have to pay emotionally later, maybe in a way that's not even worth what you received?

Does being the one who's doing the giving feel *safer* to you? I think this is the case for most of us, especially women. (For this exercise, you can write the answers in your journal or say or think them.)

Fill in the blank for this statement: "I feel safer giving than receiving because _____."

Let's do it again, digging deeper into your feelings each time:
"I feel safer giving than receiving because _____."
"I feel safer giving than receiving because _____."
"I feel safer giving than receiving because _____."

To go even deeper, think of someone from whom you might receive, and say, "I feel safer giving to (name of person) than receiving from (same name) because _____."

Remember, just bringing things into the light of your awareness begins the transformation process.

Stay in touch with the beauty of your heart as you look at your own reasons for not receiving!

RECEIVING & GIVING

As you look at things that may be in the way of your own opening to receive, always remember that safety is at the heart of this issue. Since we often don't feel completely worthy, it makes sense that deep down, we're sometimes afraid to receive!

What we need to do is bring the power of our hearts into play. I'm going to ask you to feel the energy of two different things with this exercise:

First, imagine that you're with a friend who has just done a favor for you. Feel the energy of receiving that favor, while in the back of your mind planning to do something nice for your friend in exchange. Take a moment to get a sense of what that feels like.

Now feel the energy of having that friend do you a favor and, without needing to "balance the scales," just opening your heart and letting in the love that the favor symbolizes. How does it feel to simply receive that love?

Do you feel a sense of release, or does it feel dangerous? Spend some time practicing feeling safe while opening to the feeling of the second example.

Being open to receive means living from the love in your own heart, allowing *that* to be more of a guiding force than the rules you've been taught—and trusting that the Universe loves you.

If you bring yourself back into a place of internal balance, your receiving and giving will be in a state of flow that naturally comes forth from the love in your heart—the love you have for other people, and the love you now have for yourself.

From a place of balance, your giving won't be something you do because you're following the rules or you *should* do it or you're afraid *not* to do it.

It will be a spontaneous and natural expression of what you would *love* to do in the moment. Our guidance always comes "in the moment," and as you know, I believe our guidance comes not as a feeling of what we *should* do, but as a feeling of what we would *love* to do.

Start noticing how the issue of worthiness may be tied to your own receiving, and practice living from that second example. Open your heart to receive the Source love that flows to you through other people without needing to feel safe by reciprocating or paying for it.

This is a big deal, so know that I'm sending you love and seeing you opening to receive all the good the Universe is holding out to you!

EVOLVING & EXPANDING

Let's return to a question from earlier in this chapter: When you receive, who do you believe you are receiving from? This is an all-important question when it comes to receiving.

As you know, I believe the purpose of life is to bring the energy of love into physical form.

Each one of us is spiritually evolving and expanding as we create and experience more and more of what we love, and our spiritual expansion blesses the world and everyone in it.

The things we receive are really just physical manifestations of things we've first created in energetic form, and as we experience them in physical form, we add to the richness and beauty of life.

So even though it may seem that something is coming to us from a particular person, that thing is actually coming to us from the loving, expanding Universe *through* that person.

The more you open to receive, the more you step into the flow of expansion, and once you are in that flow, giving and receiving begin to occur within a natural balance.

Most of us spend a lot of time sharing our gifts with the world, without realizing how much we are giving. When we also allow ourselves to receive, it strengthens and balances us, making each one of us a more powerful light in the world.

Shine your light more brightly now, knowing that the good you receive comes to you from Source, and when you receive that good, you create an ever-growing circle of love and light.

A DIVINE AGREEMENT BETWEEN YOU AND SOURCE

It's time to access the power of your house of self-love and let it support you as you open to receive all the good the Universe has for you.

Start by taking a deep breath, allowing your body to relax. Connect to Source love, and connect to the love the Earth has for you.

Now imagine the beautiful, strong, energetic house around you, a house representing all the self-love you are meant to have.

Feel the house's foundation forming a strong energetic support under you, and feel the strength of that love holding and supporting you. Center yourself within this energy of love surrounding you, connect to your own heart energy, and say, "I love myself."

Within this house, tune in to your heart. Feel your energetic roots to the Earth connecting and welcoming you in the world, and at the same time feel Source love pouring into you from above, filling you with life.

Feel Guardian Trees forming a circle of love around you and your house, and feel the presence of your Guardian Unicorns standing on either side of you. From this place of sacred balance, tune in to the energy of your heart, and say, "I am open to receive Source love."

Staying within your house of self-love, bring to mind some of the things you would love to experience, and say, "I am open to receive all the good that Source is flowing to me."

Take this statement seriously. Receiving is a divine agreement between you and Source, and the things you would love to receive play an important part in the natural expansion of the gifts you are here to share with the world.

Get in touch with the beauty of those gifts as you go through each day, and continue to deepen your relationship with the energy of receiving!

CHAPTER 12

FIND YOUR TRUE VOICE

This chapter is all about finding your true voice. This is so important, because the world needs to hear *your* personal truth.

We grow up thinking that we have to conform in order to be accepted, and we tend to carry that belief with us into our relationships. We use up our precious energy trying to fulfill the expectations of the people around us because we haven't been taught the truth about the value of our authentic opinions, our genuine feelings, and our personal truth.

Our true voice gets ignored, pushed to the back, and overlaid by a lot of other voices. But in every area of your life, you need to be able to get in touch with your true voice and express it out into the world. When you can do that in every situation, your life will begin to transform.

In this chapter we'll focus on five steps, each one leading you to your true voice while supporting you in expressing yourself in a way that feels good. This is important because sometimes we're in touch with what's true for us, but we haven't yet found a way to express it.

Each one of the steps is designed to support you in following your own guidance and taking small actions—slowly building upon a strong foundation, so that over time, you become more and more comfortable expressing yourself.

CLARITY

The first step is clarity. Being able to access exactly how you feel about any subject is always the beginning point, because in order to use your unique voice, you first have to know yourself. That's not as easy as it sounds, because we're not always in touch with how we feel.

We don't always take time to get in touch with our feelings and explore them, because we've been taught and trained to ignore our feelings in order to meet the expectations of the people around us.

Many of us were taught that our feelings are not to be trusted, and instead we should listen to the wisdom of others or follow the established rules.

So, along with this first step of clarity comes the necessary step of validating your feelings.

Begin by opening your heart to the presence of your Guardian Dragon. Feel it standing in front of you, and take a few moments to connect to its energy. Feel the heart of this Dragon reaching out to your own heart, and open yourself to receive its love and wisdom.

Now, with the love of your Guardian Dragon within your heart, awaken to the fact that your feelings have real value. There is truth contained within them, and this truth creates a valuable guidance system. Sit with this thought for a few moments.

Sometimes I have feelings I'm not comfortable with or that I'm even embarrassed of, but I've learned to validate them, because I know they are leading me toward a truth. Allow yourself to feel the truth of *your* own feelings now.

I try to tune in to my feelings as often as I can. In the heat of the moment, I may only have time to take note of what I'm feeling; then later when I'm alone, I take time to explore the feelings and get to the heart of what's contained inside them. The important thing is that I do this with the belief that my feelings have value and that they are *valid*.

I have to trust that I'm not just being "irrational" or "oversensitive" (or any of the other words that are used to invalidate us and our feelings). I've learned to support myself *and* whatever the feeling is, and get to the heart of it—even if it shows me something I don't like.

By doing this, I've gained some valuable insights about myself. I've learned how to get to the heart of what's really going on with me in any situation, and once I have that awareness, I'm much better able to proceed in a way that truly fulfills my needs.

Validate your feelings, give yourself permission to explore them, and trust what you find!

INTENTION

The second step on the path to finding your true voice is to identify your intention. Knowing your core intention in every situation is a powerful key to finding and using your true voice.

As you know, we spend a lot of our time reacting to what's going on around us. But when we're in reacting mode, we're not in creative mode! So it's worth taking time to stop and get back in touch with what your *core* intention is in every situation.

In an ideal world, we would consciously set forth into every situation with our intention for that situation in mind, but of course most of the time we get caught up in conversations and situations without getting a chance to get centered first.

So, when you find yourself in a situation that's not working for you, and you're not feeling able to express yourself in a way that feels good and right and effective, stop and get back in touch with your core intention. Ask yourself, "What am I trying to create here? What is my highest vision for this situation?"

For example, let's say you're having a conversation with sibling. During—if possible—or after this conversation, ask yourself, "What am I trying to create within this relationship?" (I use this example because it's something that comes up for me a lot!)

Make sure you're connecting to your intention in *positive* terms (not that you're intending to simply cope with what's going on). Instead, focus on what you are trying to create within the *core* of this relationship. For instance, with my own siblings, my intention is to create safe space within which we can love and support one another.

As you do this, it's important to remember that you can only create *your* part in it. Focus on what you would really love to see happen in the relationship, and keep that in the forefront of your mind. Know that if you keep true to that vision in your own mind, *that* is what you will be creating in energetic form—even if the other person isn't trying to create the same thing.

As long as you're in alignment with the vision of what you want to create, *that* is what you will be creating, and even if it doesn't show up in a final version within that relationship, it will send ripples throughout every part of your life and show up in some other wonderful way.

COURAGE

The third step on the path to finding your true voice has to do with courage—learning to support yourself in speaking your truth. The best place to start is to look at the thing that makes it so hard for us to express ourselves—our need for approval.

The desire to fit in and avoid conflict is pretty strong in most of us. We haven't been taught ways to express ourselves that feel safe. Even when you've gotten clear on your personal truth and tuned in to what you're intending to create, it takes courage to begin to support yourself in speaking your truth and believing in the value of what you have to say.

So here is something to hold in your heart as you move forward: *any conversation you're involved in is imbalanced without your true voice.*

This is true whether it involves several people or just two people, because the world needs to hear your truth. Your truth is valuable, your truth is important, and your truth is a *necessary component* in every situation you find yourself in.

No one can bring forth your truth except you. When you do, you support others in speaking their own truths (which they're often not doing for the same reasons we just talked about).

For now, allow yourself to take baby steps.

Let a situation come into your mind right now, a situation where you feel you're not expressing yourself authentically or where you feel you don't have a voice. Take a moment to get in touch with some of the reasons you don't feel safe expressing yourself.

Feel your Guardian Dragon before you, and open your heart to its support.

Now allow yourself to play with the idea that the conversation is not complete without your true voice included in it. Begin to integrate the idea that the world needs to hear your true voice. Sit with that idea for a few moments, still feeling the support of your Dragon Guardian.

When you tap into your truth and express it, that truth contains within it a decidedly different energy than most of the communication that goes on—and everyone can feel it. There's a power that's palpable when someone taps into their own emotional truth, even when it's not pretty.

If you begin to consciously look at the places where you're afraid to speak your truth, you may see there are good reasons that you are afraid. So don't feel you have to force yourself to all of a sudden speak up.

Instead, just hold the thought in your mind that your voice is needed in the conversation—that the other people involved would benefit from hearing your true voice whether they like what you're saying or not—and know that you're providing a valuable service to the world when you express that truth.

Just know this without having to do anything about it yet, because your knowing begins a process that will unfold in its own beautiful way and support you when you do feel ready to express your truth out loud.

Today, thank your Dragon Guardian, and remember that the small steps you take impact the world in a real way, because they lead to lasting, positive change—change that brings you more and more into alignment with your own divine nature.

SELF-TRUST

For step four, we'll circle back to the energy of self-trust, because trusting yourself supports you in expressing your emotional truth. I love this phrase: *emotional truth*.

For me, this phrase is so important because there are many situations when we feel a particular way, but we're not comfortable expressing it because we're afraid we're not *correct* in feeling the way we do.

I like to call it your emotional truth, because it doesn't have to be "correct" or right. It's just how you feel, and you can express it as such. There's such peace in that! There's such empowerment in just being able to state your emotional truth and stay in alignment with it.

Stating how we feel doesn't mean that we're trying to force it on anyone, it just means that we're willing to own it: "This is how I feel. I may learn things at a later date that change the way I feel, but right now, this is the way I feel."

Take a moment to let the power of those words sink into your being.

I believe in your emotional truth. I believe it is a powerful guide as you walk your authentic path. And I believe that when you allow yourself to get separated from your own emotional truth, you leave your path—and you start to get lost.

When something doesn't feel right to us in a situation, it's because something *isn't* right. We may then proceed to make assumptions as to the cause of our feeling—and the assumptions we make may turn out to be true or not—but the fact that *something* is causing our gut feeling is irrefutable.

So from now on, refuse to allow anything to separate you from your own self-trust. Know that by trusting your own instincts, you're helping to create situations that are healthier and safer for everyone involved.

Being able to express how you feel without needing to justify or defend it is a powerful thing!

CREATIVITY

Part of developing your true voice is the practice of expressing yourself, and that brings us to step five, the energy of creativity: expressing your unique self in *everything* you do.

Each one of us is so wonderfully unique, but we pass up so many opportunities to express our unique self in the world!

Everything you do is an opportunity to use your creativity to express your authentic, capital-*S* Self in the world. Your surroundings, what you eat, how you dress, your handwriting, the words you use—there are countless ways in which you can express the beautiful self that is you. Start taking advantage of these opportunities today.

Creatively expressing your unique self brings so much more life force into your being, because at our essence, we are all creators. You empower yourself when you express yourself consciously in every way, because you're sending yourself the message that your unique self is important, that it's valuable, and that it's worth expressing in everything you do.

This makes you energetically *bigger*. When you allow yourself to believe that your true self is beautiful and valuable and worth expressing in all its quirky ways, you become stronger and more whole. It also allows you to see the beauty in everyone else's expression.

Think of an area in your life where you're not creatively expressing yourself—not putting your own unique stamp on whatever it is you're doing.

Now take a nice deep breath, ground yourself down into the Earth, and connect to the love of your Guardian Dragon. Open your heart to receive inspiration about how you can more fully express yourself creatively in this part of your life.

This inspiration might come right away in the form of a new idea. You might find a scene unfolding in your mind's eye, taking you on an inner journey with your Guardian Dragon. Or you might become aware of new inspiration in the days that follow.

Keep that channel of inspiration open, and as you do, say thank you to your Guardian Dragon. Thank also the universal forces that are supporting you in creating from your heart and expressing that beautiful heart out into the world in everything you do.

Allow yourself to start small. Every situation is an opportunity for you to explore and express your true voice, and that exploration is important because the more of yourself you explore, the more beauty and magic your unique self can bring forth to bless the world.

CHAPTER 13

❧

MAKE PEACE WITH WHERE YOU ARE

Is there a place in your life where you are resisting what is? Take a moment and look within to see if there's a place where you're not accepting an unwanted truth.

It could be an unwanted truth about a relationship, your work, your family, your financial situation, or any other part of your life.

There are two ways this resistance can show up. In relationships, resistance to the truth often takes the form of *passive* denial. We might be less than happy, but afraid to admit it to ourselves.

We numb ourselves to how the situation makes us feel, and that numbing becomes a problem in itself, because when we numb ourselves to one thing, we become more and more numb to everything—and we get cut off from our own wisdom and guidance.

Resisting what is can also take the form of *active* denial—scrambling to *not* be in the situation you find yourself in.

It's a kind of thrashing around, panicked, afraid-of-the-future feeling—a feeling of not being able to get your bearings. When you're in this state, you're cut off from your own inner resources, because the very act of scrambling keeps you going in circles.

One of the reasons we resist what's going on in the present is that we're afraid the current situation will keep us from having what we want in the future. We worry that accepting where we are will mean resigning ourselves to an ongoing, unhappy situation.

But the opposite is true! Only by accepting what is can we begin to change it.

When you can't accept the reality of your life as it is right now, you pour your valuable energy into a pattern of resistance that actually serves to keep you stuck.

But once you can accept your situation—whatever it is—you can begin to move forward.

So the first step here is just to be willing to look within. See if there are places in your life where you're not accepting the truth of what is, and if there are, don't worry!

Within you, you have everything you need to create the life that's right for you. Hold that thought in your heart.

STEPPING STONES

The second step in making peace with where you are is to consider the idea that your *resistance* (not the situation itself) is the problem. I know, this is hard!

Life is a continual process of improvement: trying things out, seeing what results we get, and starting over, always focusing our attention on what we *want*.

You have the inner resources to improve any situation you find yourself in, but in order to access those resources, you first have to stop trying *not* to be where you are.

When I was growing up, disaster movies were popular. In these films, some traumatic event would suddenly befall a group of people. In every case, one or more of these people would immediately panic, not accepting where they were or what had happened. They would freak out and thrash around and be no help at all.

Then there was the hero of the movie. (In those days it was always a man.) The first step on the hero's path would be to accept that the traumatic event had happened—they *were* stuck in the tunnel or the burning building or the sinking ship or wherever.

They were where they were. And with that as his starting point, the hero of the story was always able to find a way *out* of where they were.

But the people who freaked out and couldn't accept where they were didn't do so well.

Try to apply this to whatever is going on in your life right now, big or small. Instead of trying to go back to a place in the past, beating yourself up for where you are now, or feeling that where you are now means you can't get to where you want to be, accept where you are, knowing that *where you are can lead you to where you want to be.*

Where you are doesn't have to be an insurmountable obstacle.

Once you allow yourself to make peace with the fact of where you are, you can access your inner guidance, your inner wisdom, and the help that's all around you. Your current situation *can* be a stepping stone to where you are meant to be.

RECONNECT TO YOUR EMPOWERMENT

Whenever you're having trouble making peace with where you are, the parts of your identity that aren't built on your true, authentic self will make themselves known.

The parts of your self-image that are weak or inauthentic will come to the surface during times when you're not where you want to be. This really sucks while you're going through it, but resist the urge to thrash around or beat yourself up!

During this time, you'll have the opportunity to release the parts of your self-image that don't strengthen you and rebuild your self-image on a strong sense of who you *truly* are.

That brings us to the next step: reconnect to your own empowerment. When you believe you need things to be different before you can feel fundamentally safe, it's a signal that you're cut off from your own empowerment.

This is another opportunity to reexamine your belief system. As you know, each of us has a personal belief system, whether it's something we've created as we've gone along or a spiritual belief system that was taught to us. (Like it or not, it's usually a mix of both.)

Our belief systems directly affect the choices we make and the way we feel. They also have a *lot* to do with how safe or fearful we feel in any situation.

Look inside yourself right now. Deep down, do you feel that life is for you or against you? Within your own belief system, do you believe you can emerge from difficult times into an even better life?

If you want to believe that life is *for* you, then start consciously integrating that belief into every part of your being. Begin to live every day from the belief that life is on your side.

The more you do this, the more you'll be at peace within unwelcome situations, knowing that your life is in the process of getting better.

Practice becoming more aware of your own belief system. Notice whether it supports you in feeling safe or feeling afraid, and remember that you have the power to choose the beliefs you carry within.

THE FEAR THAT'S KEEPING YOU STUCK

As we've journeyed through this chapter, have you identified a place in your life where you don't want to accept the truth of a situation? It could be small or large, but hold it in your mind as we continue.

It's time to identify the specific fear that's keeping you stuck.

As I've noted, the reason we don't have an easy time making peace with where we are is often because we're *afraid* of where we are. We are afraid it's not safe to be where we are. There can be a lot of different, unnamed fears tangled up inside us, even when the issue is a small one.

But hear this now: when you are stuck in fear mode, you are believing something about yourself that is not true. There's *a false belief underneath the fear* that's disempowering you and keeping you stuck in place.

So if there's a place in your life where you're resisting where you are, take a deeper look now and locate the fear that's keeping you stuck.

Specifically identify what it is that's making you feel unsafe. For some people it's a feeling that they should have "succeeded" by now, and the fact that they haven't yet succeeded means that it's not possible for them.

You might be beating yourself up for decisions you've made in the past, and your underlying fear is that these bad decisions have made it impossible for you to have lasting happiness.

Or you might feel that you should have what you want by now, and that you must not be good enough to *deserve* to live your dreams.

These are all false beliefs. They're all based on things that are untrue: untrue about you, untrue about what you are capable of, untrue about what you're meant to have, and untrue about how much support you have available to you.

Identify your fear and then identify the false belief that's keeping the fear alive by reflecting on the following prompts, then writing your answers in a journal.

Think of and describe a part of your life where you are resisting what is.

Tune in to how this situation makes you feel. Jot down words that describe the feelings.

Sift through the feelings until you find the fear at their core. I am afraid that: _____.

Now identify and describe the false belief that's fueling your fear.

If the false belief still feels true, call upon your Guardian Unicorns. Feel them standing on either side of you, and in the light of their presence, allow this false belief to be replaced with the truth.

STABILIZE & MOVE FORWARD TO A BETTER PLACE

In order to move forward to someplace better, you need to first make peace with where you are so that you can stabilize yourself.

When you're not making peace with where you are, your personal vibration is one of fear and resistance. When you are attracting from that vibration, what you tend to attract are more things that cause you to be fearful—more things that aren't working out the way you want them to—and this can easily turn into a downward spiral.

Make peace with where you are and stabilize yourself. When I google the word *stabilize*, I find these definitions: "make (or become) unlikely to give way or overturn" and "make (or become) unlikely to change, fail, or decline." (Parentheses mine.)

I'm going to repeat these definitions because I think just hearing them can begin to change our own energy: "become unlikely to give way or overturn" and "become unlikely to change, fail, or decline."

When you find yourself resisting where you are, repeat the word *stabilize* to yourself.

Stabilize.

Stabilize.

Stabilize.

Remember that the Earth has its own soul, and the powerful, loving being that is the Earth is creating a strong, *stable* foundation for you to build your life upon.

Drop your roots into the Earth and let them sink deeply and spread out widely. Relax into where you are, stabilize by bringing yourself back to your own powerful center, and allow the Universe to support you in turning your focus to a direction of hope and positive expectation.

With that as your focus, all sorts of new opportunities and new ideas will become visible to you.

ADOPT A NEW MINDSET

The next step in making peace with where you are is to adopt a new mindset. This is a pivotal step, and over time, it can change everything!

It starts with adopting a new motto. This motto is: *everything always works out for me.*

For some people this motto is very foreign, and for others it comes more easily. Either way, allow yourself to stop and let the energy of these words soak into your being.

You may not have had a life where you feel that everything always worked out for you, but that can change now. The Universe is supporting you in getting better and better at focusing on what you love and bringing it forth into the world.

That includes your work, your family, your finances—every part of your life can change when you align yourself with the energy of ever-expanding, positive outcomes.

No matter what's going on in your life at any given time, return to your motto: everything always works out for me.

That mindset paves the way for good things to come into your present situation, things that you won't have access to if you're focusing on what you fear.

Imagine standing on a path, facing either in one direction or another. Whichever direction you are facing is where you are heading. If you're resisting where you are, feeling unsafe, and scrambling around (or numbing yourself), then you're not faced in the direction of where you want to go.

But when you can get some hope in your heart, when you can relax, when you can allow yourself to tap into the love of your Guardians and the power coming to you from Source, then you can begin to believe—a little bit at first and then more and more—*everything always works out for me.* Then you are faced in the other direction, heading toward the life you most want to create.

When I experienced the financial losses I told you about in our Preface, it was a real test of this motto. Not only did I lose the house I'd owned for 26 years, but I then moved into my parents' second living room, with a big curtain instead of a door.

The complete lack of privacy, the shame of my financial situation, and the job where I was supervised by teenagers—it was a perfect storm of humiliation, and the very definition of where I *didn't* want to be in life.

And sometimes it did bring me to a very dark place emotionally. But my strong sense of soul purpose and my belief that "everything always works out for me" acted as a powerful compass, turning me time and time again to face in the direction of my dreams.

So adopt this new mindset for yourself today: *everything always works out for me*. We'll be expanding on this thought in Chapter 26, but start now to incorporate this belief in everything you do.

No matter what is happening right now, it is *not* more powerful than you. You can create the life that's right for you no matter where you are now, but you need to be pointed in the direction of that better life in order to experience it.

> *Close your eyes, take a deep breath, relax, and feel yourself surrounded by Angelic energy. Call on your Guardian Angel, the holder of the pattern for the perfect unfolding of your life.*
>
> *Think of your present situation, and feel the presence of your Guardian Angel behind you, shining pure white light into your body.*
>
> *Feel this light shine through the back of your body and head, and as it moves through you, see this light projected into the space before you as a movie. Your Guardian Angel is bringing light and life through your own divine blueprint, and shining it, through you, into the world for you to see now.*
>
> *As you watch this movie, see yourself living as you are meant to live, completely in alignment with your Greater Self and your soul purpose.*
>
> *What do you see?*
>
> *How does it make you feel?*
>
> *Anchor these feelings in your body as you ground into the love of the Earth, thanking your Guardian Angel.*
>
> *Keep the movie and your Guardian Angel in your awareness as you open your eyes. Write down everything you saw and felt in the movie, and repeat this process often. Feel yourself naturally coming more and more into alignment with the movie as you release your fears and step into the manifestation of your divine blueprint now.*

If you choose it, everything always works out for you. Make peace with your current situation, then begin to expect positive change, no matter where you are.

CHAPTER 14

~✦~

UPGRADE YOUR SELF-TALK

Our self-talk is made up of what we say to ourselves all day long, a running monologue under the surface of our awareness. It reflects our personal patterns of thinking and the "programs" that are active within us.

Most of us have heard the same thoughts inside our heads for so long that we accept them as truth—a very deep form of truth. That's what makes negative self-talk so debilitating: we believe it so deeply.

In this chapter we'll become more aware of our own self-talk, and as we do, we'll reconnect with our power to consciously choose how we want to speak to ourselves.

Tune in now and ask yourself: "What types of things have you been saying to yourself so far today?"

As you reflect, focus on the energy of your own heart and hold yourself in a space of self-love. Feel yourself a welcomed, beloved part of the Earth, and know that you have all the power you need to transform your self-talk into something that matches the power of your own beautiful heart.

Your self-talk is a major factor in the quality of your life. Let's bring it to the surface now and transform it into the positive force it's meant to be.

117

BECOME FULLY AWARE OF YOUR SELF-TALK

Upgrading your self-talk can improve your life dramatically, so set an intention now to become *fully* aware of your own inner monologue.

Think back to the last time you felt anxious. What negative messages do you think might have been playing in your mind at that time? In other words, what thoughts must you have been believing in order to feel so anxious?

Take a few moments to identify the under-the-surface self-talk that was creating, contributing to, or supporting your anxiety.

Now give yourself a moment to reexamine those thoughts. Do you truly believe them?

Think back to the last time you felt embarrassed. What negative messages do you think might have been playing in your mind at that time? In other words, what thoughts must you have been believing in order to feel embarrassed?

Take a few moments to identify the under-the-surface self-talk that was creating, contributing to, or supporting your embarrassment.

Give yourself a moment to reexamine those thoughts. Do you truly believe them?

Now think back to the last time you felt really, really good. Recall and relive those feelings in your body, mind, and spirit.

What positive messages do you think might have been playing in your mind at that time? In other words, what thoughts must you have been believing in order to feel so good?

Take a few moments to identify the under-the-surface self-talk that was creating, contributing to, or supporting your well-being.

Pay attention to the way you feel from now on, and take regular time to stop and identify the self-talk that's supporting or undermining you.

START SAYING SUPPORTIVE THINGS TO YOURSELF

Someone I know used to work for a floral designer, and she told me a story about him that has really stayed with me.

They were setting up the floral arrangements for a big, important wedding, and everything was going wrong—they didn't have the correct supplies, and part of the staff hadn't shown up. They were working frantically, trying to set up the floral displays before they ran out of time. The crew heard their boss speaking to himself out loud as he worked.

"You can do this," he said to himself, over and over. And it was true. As always, everything turned out looking great.

The story stuck with me because it was a real-life example of how supporting ourselves actually works. Think of how your own life might change if you started saying supportive things to yourself, all day long!

Some of your self-talk can take the form of reminding yourself of what you already know to be true.

For example, when my daughter, Jenny, moved to San Francisco a few years ago, I found myself driving into the city on a regular basis for the first time in my life.

I was raised in the suburbs, and driving in San Francisco (with all the hills and unfamiliar freeways) intimidated me. On one of my early trips to visit Jenny, I noticed myself feeling really anxious in the traffic as I navigated through the city.

So as I drove, I started talking to myself in my mind. "It's just driving. You know how to drive, Kim. You've been driving for over forty years! It doesn't matter if you know the area or not. No matter where you are, you know how to drive!"

It was true! And it made such a difference.

I'd like to ask you to go out of your way to support yourself in this same way. Say something supportive to yourself at least four times today, and take a moment to notice how it feels. Notice how you feel in your body, and take note of any resistance that might come up.

Take a moment at the end of the day to assess the cumulative effect of your positive self-talk. Say something supportive to yourself as you drift off to sleep, and as you do, remember that I'm sending you love!

YOUR PERSONAL FAIRY GODMOTHER

I believe that each of us should stay aware of and upgrade our own self-talk on an ongoing basis for the rest of our lives. It's that important!

It's as if you have someone you trust whispering in your ear every day, and too often, it can feel like that someone is whispering scary things all day long.

So call in a special Guardian to elevate your inner monologue.

Start by recognizing your own value and power by centering yourself within your house of self-love and saying, "I love myself."

Open to the presence of your Greater Self, and feel it fill you and spread out to fill your house of self-love. Feel the presence of wise old Trees encircling your house of self-love.

Tune in to your own energy field, and call all your energy back into your body. Drop energetic roots down into the Earth, and feel love and support flowing up to envelop you. Focus on the energy of your own heart, and feel your own beautiful "energy signature."

Now imagine that you have your own personal "Fairy Godmother." (I believe the energy of the Fairy Godmother has always existed as a living Guardian Being, and over the centuries, we have strengthened our connection to her through our stories and fairy tales.)

Imagine that this Fairy Godmother isn't allowed to use her magic on your behalf. Instead, she's here to help awaken you to your own personal magic, your own creative power, and your own magnificent wisdom.

Feel her presence with you now, and spend a few moments listening to what she has to say to you.

Think back again to the last time you felt anxious. Bring to mind the negative self-talk that was fueling your anxiety. What does your Fairy Godmother have to say to you about this?

Now think back again to the last time you felt embarrassed. Bring to mind the negative self-talk that was fueling your embarrassment.

What does your Fairy Godmother have to say about that?

Now think of something you really, really want to do, be, or have. What does your Fairy Godmother have to say to you?

Anchor this wisdom within you. Continue to call forth your Fairy Godmother, and tune in to what she has to say to you. Absorb this special wisdom into your heart, and allow it to transform your self-talk.

WHAT KIND OF SELF-TALK WOULD YOU NEED?

Think of three things you really, really want to do, be, or have. Take a moment to get them into your mind.

Bring the first thing into your mind, and spend a few moments with this question: "What kind of self-talk would you need to have in order to be the person who is doing, being, or having this thing?"

Now bring the second thing into your mind, and spend a few moments with this question: "What kind of self-talk would you need to have in order to be the person who is doing, being, or having this thing?"

And now bring the third thing into your mind, and spend a few moments with this question: "What kind of self-talk would you need to have in order to be the person who is doing, being, or having this thing?"

Be prepared to take notes and jot down any thoughts that come to you as you continue to ask yourself these questions, and allow your

Fairy Godmother to help you access the truths you need in order to be able to fulfill your own divine blueprint and live out your visions.

RECONNECT WITH A DEEPER WISDOM

Connecting with a Fairy Godmother has allowed us to connect with feminine wisdom, and in the following guided journey, we'll balance that by connecting to masculine wisdom as well.

Take a deep, slow breath, and allow yourself to sink into your furniture as you feel a wave of relaxation flowing through you. Feel this wave of energy clearing and cleansing, relaxing and releasing every part of your body from the top of your head down into your chest, through your hips and legs, all the way out your feet.

As you relax and go within, you begin to see yourself inside a beautiful, cozy room. Something about this room makes you feel warm and safe, and you feel the warmth and safety of this space filling every part of you.

On one wall of this room there is a big fireplace, and sitting in front of the fire is a wise old man. He welcomes you, and you immediately know that you can trust him. In fact, you feel better just being in his presence.

He asks you to sit by the fire, and as you do, you think of a problem you're currently facing. You tell the wise old man about your problem, and you tell him how your problem makes you feel about yourself.

He listens intently, and when you are done speaking, he takes your hands and looks deeply into your eyes. You sit quietly as he communicates to you the deeper truth in your situation.

You open your heart and mind to soak in the wisdom, love, and support in this message. You feel a new appreciation for yourself, and you take this appreciation deeply into yourself.

From now on you will let your own voice of love and support replace any negative self-talk. Your feelings and experiences will change for the better in every situation as you tune in to this wisdom within.

And any time you feel unsure, you can return to this place and soak in the warmth, safety, and truth you find here, reconnecting to the deeper wisdom that is always supporting you in your own unique truth and your own unique beauty.

When you feel ready, take a deep breath and come back to your normal waking state.

I'm holding space for you to hear a new voice come forth from within you, a loving voice based on your own truth and wisdom. Turn toward this voice!

CHAPTER 15

✦

RELEASE THE PAST

In order to be completely grounded in the present (with access to our full empowerment), we need to free ourselves from ideas and beliefs we've outgrown. Even more importantly, we need to *make peace* with our own personal histories, so now we'll focus on releasing the past.

Releasing the past can take many forms: releasing old relationships, releasing old vows, releasing old goals, and releasing old dreams. This isn't always easy, because letting go is hard! So be gentle with yourself. Just *thinking* about the ideas we'll be working with in this chapter is enough to begin a positive change inside you.

Most of us are carrying around a burden of leftover things from our past—things we haven't been able to come to terms with, in addition to negative emotions—that hold us back from creating what we want to create today.

We're not always conscious of carrying this excess baggage, but there's an easy way to tell if something from your past needs to be released or transformed. If, when you think of a situation in your past, you feel an immediate negative emotion, then you are carrying a very real energetic burden.

This negative emotion needs to be transformed so that you can reclaim your empowerment, reclaim the pieces of yourself that you left behind, and move forward in creative mode.

I believe we create and attract things into our lives based on the energy that's activated within us in the present. But so many times what's active within us is the energy of old, unresolved issues from our past! This is because, deep down, we're still trying to figure out where we went wrong.

It's as if we have a splinter that works its way in and never gets removed. It stays there under the surface. We don't always notice it, but when something pushes against it and triggers it, our painful, unresolved feelings flare up.

The things that cause us pain are the *meanings* we give to events, and not the events themselves, so in this chapter we'll set a new intention to find truer, hope-filled meanings in the events of your past as we explore ways to set yourself free and move forward with clarity, peace, and passion.

Know that you have the power to transform and reclaim your own beautiful energy now as you release the past.

TRANSFORMING THE ENERGY OF THE PAST

One of the things we're traditionally taught is that we should learn from our past, but it seems to me that a lot of the things that we learn from our past are fear-based lessons that don't reflect the truth of our being. We learn not to trust, we learn not to relax and be ourselves, and we learn not to expect the best.

Let's consider a new way of thinking. My understanding of one of the Law of Attraction teachings from Abraham-Hicks is that when you experience something painful or unpleasant, the *opposite* of that painful experience is created in energetic form: something better that matches who you're truly meant to be.

We can apply this concept to everything that's happened in our past. Every time you experienced something painful, a new, happier possibility was created. The energy of painful and disappointing experiences from your past may still be carried in your heart—but happy, satisfying, and fulfilling potentials are carried there too.

The problem is, we tend to keep focusing on the things that didn't turn out, and so the energy of old, unwanted outcomes stays active within us in the present.

We can use the example of a relationship that didn't last or wasn't everything you wanted it to be—a relationship that contained some good things but also a lot of unhappiness. From now on, you can release the things that weren't the way you wanted them to be by focusing on the *better* things that have been created for you in response to the things that caused you pain.

Invoking your house of self-love as you go through your day will help with this. The more you actively love yourself, the more you'll notice a change within yourself in terms of what you feel you deserve, and it will be easier and easier to release the pain of the past and believe that you are *meant* to enjoy new, better experiences.

It would actually be best if we were able to completely release our attachment to the past and allow ourselves to be freshly born with unlimited possibilities in every new moment. But the negative emotions we carry from our past keep us connected to it, so our focus right now is on transforming the energy of the past so that it empowers us rather than weakening us.

This means keeping the fulfilling, empowering parts of your past active within you, knowing that good outcomes that are right for you have *already* been created for you.

They are waiting for you in energetic form, and the more you believe in them and bring your energy into alignment with them, the more you'll begin to experience them in physical form.

BE YOUR OWN ADVOCATE

Everything you've experienced in the past can be seen as a series of puzzle pieces, with all the pieces coming together now to create a happy life. I believe this is how it's meant to be for all of us, so together, let's give the events of the past—those puzzle pieces in *your* life—a new meaning.

If you feel guilt or shame about mistakes you've made in the past is holding you back, do some reframing of those events with me.

We've probably all had the experience of watching a movie and being very engaged with the lead character (even if she isn't a very heroic lead character).

In the movie, we watch her go through a lot of ups and downs, and we are right there with her on that journey because we're seeing things through her eyes.

Because we are right by her side as the movie goes on, we *understand* the choices she makes. We may not agree with them or even support them—and sometimes when she's making these decisions, we're thinking, *Aw no, don't do* that!—but even while we're thinking that, *we understand why she's doing it.* We understand why she's making that "mistake," because we've seen everything that has led up to it.

I'm going to challenge you now to give yourself that same support and understanding.

In the movie analogy, we are on the lead character's side. We want her to succeed, and we believe she can. We see the mistakes and missteps she's made, but *we believe in her ability to create a happy ending, regardless of her past.*

So consider being on your own side when you look back at your past from now on.

We tend to only look back at the results of our actions or the big mistakes we think we've made or the things we've done that we feel guilty or ashamed about; we don't take into account the big picture or the events that led us to feel that was the choice we *had* to make.

So just assume there was sense in what you did in your past. Assume that if you could go back and relive it—while being your own advocate—you would understand. You might still want to make a different choice, but you wouldn't be blaming yourself the way you are now.

From now on, *join me in being on your side.* If we remember the Law of Attraction principle I mentioned earlier, we know that when the consequences from our decisions were not the things we'd hoped for, they caused something new to be created.

From those negative experiences, positive possibilities came into being, and those new possibilities are just waiting for you to experience them. So take your focus off your guilt or the mistakes you feel you've made.

When you do, you'll take away their power to affect you in the present and future. Reclaim the power to create a wonderful life regardless of what has happened in the past—whether it was something that was done to you or something you did.

Give yourself a clean slate right now from which to create, and know that as you do, the Universe is supporting you.

RELEASING OLD GOALS

As you release and transform your feelings about the past, you may come across other things that need to be released from your inner landscape. One of those things is old goals.

You may be carrying around goals that you've outgrown: goals you've taken on from authority figures, goals you've taken on from your family, and even goals you've taken on from your culture.

These old goals are probably not active in your daily consciousness; they just simmer on the back burner of your mind, creating a nagging feeling that there's something you should have gotten done by now or something that you *still* need to get done.

What happened in the past affects our sense of identity today, and that's part of what makes it so hard to release the past. In a way, we feel we *are* our past, that our past is what makes us, *us*.

Take this moment to remind yourself that this isn't true. There's a bigger, deeper, more authentic Self that is who you *truly* are. You're not the things you have experienced—you are a deeper, wiser, eternal being. The things you've experienced have served to help you create better things. *That* is the true value of the past.

Begin to get in alignment with the true value of the things you have experienced in the past. Reclaim your empowerment and reclaim (or rather, claim for the first time) all the wonderful new things that were energetically created by everything you've experienced in the past.

Firmly put your focus on what you love, and empower yourself to believe in a whole new chapter in your life. Begin this chapter knowing that life doesn't have to be a struggle.

Base your belief about what's possible purely on what you love and what you would love to see happen, and not on what has happened in the past. Believe in the reality of the things that feel good to you and believe they are meant for you, even if they haven't shown up yet.

In this way life continues to expand and evolve. When you release the old goals that really aren't *you* anymore, you can begin to create from a deeper, truer part of yourself. New doors will open up, new possibilities will make their way to you, and new projects will spark your passion.

By getting rid of goals you've outgrown, you'll have much greater access to your own energy—and that will show up as a feeling of passion in the moment.

RELEASING OLD VOWS

As we focus on releasing the past, it's important to include releasing ourselves from old vows.

Our wedding vows usually contain the words, "Till death do us part," and if we've been married and divorced, sometimes we continue to carry around our old wedding vows without realizing it.

Vows are a huge deal! We make them with great sincerity, and they are genuine. Wedding vows come straight from our hearts, so it's no wonder they can still be active within us, even years after we've been divorced.

And this doesn't just apply to wedding vows. We make similar (unspoken) vows in the workplace and with family members.

So allow yourself to release the vows that you no longer *choose* to fulfill. Keep the positive intention with which you made the vow, and know that the positive intention can't be taken from you. The essence of the positive intentions of the past are something you can continue to keep activated within you and add to as you move forward to bring more and more love into your life.

We also may need to release the old dreams that went along with past relationships or situations. Often what's hardest to come to terms with when a relationship ends is the dream you had when you began the relationship. Any project or phase of our lives is begun with a dream, and when that phase comes to a disappointing end, the hardest part is often releasing the dream we had in the beginning.

We cling to old dreams because we think if we let go of a specific dream, there will be nothing left in its place but disappointment. But in the supportive energy we share here together, you can release your unfulfilled dreams, keeping what was positive about them and knowing that a better, fuller version of the dream is possible for you now.

Take a deep breath now and bring it all the way into your center. Feel the love in your heart shining bright, and know that it's safe now to release old dreams.

Feel the presence of your Guardian Unicorn walking at your side while your Guardian Dragon leads you forward into a space filled with golden light.

Know that your old dreams have already evolved and are waiting for you to step into them now.

Don't feel you have to do this all at once. Just let my words sink in, and open yourself to the idea that you can be free of old vows and old disappointments.

RELEASING OUR PAST IDENTIFICATIONS

Life is meant to get better and better as you create more and more of what you love, and releasing the past sets us free to do that. So let's look at some physical signs that let you know your self-image may be tied to the past.

Sometimes we try to strengthen our self-image with physical things we feel give us more value. Think about your own clothing and the physical things you keep around you, and notice what's current—which items are totally in line with the life you are living right now—and which items are tied to a self-image you used to have (or a self-image you *wanted* to have).

Look around with fresh eyes, and if you notice outgrown things you're holding on to, take a deep breath and recognize that they don't have anything to do with the *true* you.

Set yourself free from identification with things that don't reflect your true self. If you find you're not in *active* relationship with clothing or other objects—if they don't really express who you are today—consider releasing them.

Be forewarned that doing so may bring up emotions that are tied to all the things we've talked about in this chapter. So be patient with yourself, and use the outdated physical objects around you to *gently* work through the process of releasing.

Expect more and more goodness to come into your life as you let yourself release the old things that really don't fit or that no longer serve you.

Allow yourself to change and evolve now by releasing the past. It doesn't need to exist anymore.

CALLING YOUR ENERGY BACK

Now let's go within to reclaim the parts of ourselves that may have been lost in the past.

Take in a nice deep breath, and as you slowly exhale, open your heart to the Goddess Isis. To me, Isis is the Great Mother, and She will hold you in her arms as you go within to release the past.

Feel yourself safely held within the loving arms of Isis now, and see beautiful rose-pink energy rising like a mist around you both. Breathe in this light rose-pink color until you can feel it in every part of your body.

Set an intention to call back to you only the parts of yourself that will strengthen, uplift, and complete you now.

See a large leather-bound book on a stand before you. This book contains the stories and energies of your life up to now. Feel the support and safety of Isis supporting you as you open this book and look through it.

Now speak your clear decision to reclaim your precious energy from the past. Watch as beautiful gold and pink sparkling energy begins to rise from the book.

Call this energy to you. Call it into the palms of your hands, where you can use it to fashion a present and a future that support your biggest, most powerful, and most radiant self.

Feel yourself centered, balanced, and whole as you take another deep breath, grounding into the love of the Earth, and thanking Isis.

I am sending you love as you go shining forth from now on, carrying with you the love of Isis—free from the past and ready to bestow your gifts upon the radiant future.

PART III

MOVE
FORWARD IN
A NEW WAY

This Part will help you move through each day in a whole new way, supported by your Guardians as you bring your dreams to life! As a reminder, I suggest you read the chapters in order, and then you can return to the chapters with the skills you want to work on as needed. There are exercises and meditations throughout. You can complete them in your head, read them aloud, or write them down in a journal. For a richer, guided experience, you can get my *Guardian Gateway Activation Experience*, which contains 29 videos and more than 60 illustrated transformation sheets. (Visit www.kimwilborn.com/activation-experience for more information.)

CHAPTER 16

❧

BE YOURSELF

Here are two truths: (1) only by being yourself can you be truly happy; (2) you can't be motivated by a need to please others and be yourself at the same time.

You've probably already heard that life is designed to work best when you are true to yourself. But it's easier said than done!

Most of us get trapped in a cycle of people-pleasing and approval-seeking at an early age. We learn that approval feels good, like love, and disapproval feels awful, like rejection (and a judgment that we're not good enough).

We train ourselves to people-please in order to avoid the awful feeling of disapproval and rejection, and in doing so, we give everyone in the world the power to judge whether or not we're good enough.

But remember the two truths we started with: you can't be motivated by a need to please others and be yourself at the same time, and *only by being yourself can you be truly happy*. Let's take a moment now to tap into two different states.

> *First, think of a situation where you are, or have been, worried about doing the right thing in order to fit in or be seen as good enough. As you bring the situation to mind, notice how it feels. Take note now of how this type of situation feels in your body. Think of a word or phrase that describes these feelings.*

> *Now think of a situation in which you feel safe completely being yourself, and notice how that feels. Take note now of how this type of situation feels in your body. Think of a word or phrase that describes these feelings.*

When I'm in a situation with a friend or loved one with whom I feel safe being completely myself, it feels like my spirit is set free. I can feel my energy expanding and dancing with a sense of freedom and joy. My body is completely relaxed.

You deserve to be in this second state all the time. In this chapter we'll begin a process of transformation you can return to again and again to become more and more comfortable being yourself, and more and more tapped into the energies that make you feel happy and fully alive.

Making the change will take courage on your part, but I promise you, it will be worth it!

THE SAFETY OF YOUR GREATER SELF

When you pretend to be different than you are, you weaken yourself. But when you can stand in your own unique energy knowing the *value* of your authentic way of being (quirks and all), you empower yourself—and you shine.

As always, at the core of this issue is a need to feel safe. Our goal in this chapter is to embody the truth that being ourselves is actually safer than fitting in.

Recognize the value of being who you *truly* are. You can start by beginning an ongoing practice of getting into alignment with your Greater Self, the eternal part of you that's completely aligned with the truth of your being. Staying consciously connected to your Greater Self will help you stay in a state of connection with your own unique beauty and value.

A conscious connection with your Greater Self also brings with it a powerful sense of safety, and this safety creates a stable foundation for you as you get more and more comfortable being yourself in every situation.

We all tend to think it would be better if we were less like ourselves and more like our role models. But only by being who you truly are can you manifest your unique life purpose, and only by manifesting your unique life purpose can you feel satisfied in life.

Call forth your house of self-love now, and feel its strong energetic walls around you. Say, "I love myself." Feel the ring of old, wise Trees standing around your house, and connect to their nurturing presence.

Now tune in to your own heart, and feel the presence of your Greater Self there. Open yourself to this presence and allow it to grow until it fills you, surrounds you, and stretches out to fill your house of self-love.

Notice the way it feels to embody this much of your Greater Self.

Now say again, "I love myself." Does it feel different this time?

As we commit to this transformation, we trade in the false safety of fitting in for the power we generate by being ourselves. We adopt a new goal: to be more *fully* ourselves in every moment, expressing more and more of our natural way of being in everything we do.

UNCOMFORTABLE SITUATIONS

As you focus on being yourself, your first mission is to become aware of the times when you are *not* being yourself.

Begin to notice the times when you are acting out a role or people-pleasing or changing your natural behavior to something "better." (These are all very familiar to me!) Don't worry about changing any of this; just noticing is the first step.

Think back to a situation in the recent past when you were uncomfortable being yourself. What exactly about the situation made you feel uncomfortable?

Bring the situation to life in your mind's eye now. Feel yourself within this situation once more, but this time, allow the energy of your Greater Self to fill you and spread out around you. Feel the love of the Earth supporting you.

Now bring all your energy back into your physical being and relax into the energy of your authentic self. As you do, notice what you feel in your heart.

See yourself back in this uncomfortable situation, but this time full of the power of your Greater Self, surrounded and uplifted by the love of the Earth, and relaxing into the safety of being yourself.

Now come back into the present moment, but stay connected to your Greater Self, the loving Earth, and the safety of relaxing into the real you.

As you go through the days ahead, set an intention to become aware when you're uncomfortable being yourself. Don't try to force yourself to change anything; simply repeat the process we've just gone through and realign with the support you need to return to your own authentic nature.

YOUR OWN MAGIC

Once you begin to identify the areas in which you're not being yourself, you can go deeper and discover the *reasons* you don't feel safe being yourself in those situations.

Self-knowledge leads to empowerment, so go within now and begin to get clear on the places in your life where it's hard to completely be yourself.

Once you have a few situations in mind, choose one, and look at it more deeply.

What are your underlying motives within this situation? In other words, what are you there for?

Look at your normal way of operating within this situation. Does it involve people-pleasing or the need for approval? (If so, don't feel bad. I can relate!)

Recognize that every time you do something in order to get approval, you move away from your authentic self, and in so doing, you weaken yourself.

Take the situation you brought to mind a moment ago, and take some time now to imagine different ways of being within this situation. Imagine yourself relaxing into your authentic self and feeling the stability of the Earth beneath your feet.

Allow in the presence of your Greater Self, and as you do, open yourself to your own magic. There's powerful, magical energy within you that can only be accessed and expressed when you're completely being yourself. Try out different scenarios within this situation in your mind's eye right now, until you find one you love.

Hold on to that feeling.

PAUSING TO GET CENTERED

You need to be yourself in order to be a true creator in life. So it's time to focus on getting to know who you really are in *every* moment.

Sometimes our day can feel like a runaway train, but it's actually made up of several different parts that we move through, one right after the other. Taking a moment to pause and get centered before we engage in a new focus is a powerful practice we can use to return to who we truly are.

Picture the events of yesterday morning. Can you break down your morning into four or five distinct parts? An example might be: prepared and ate breakfast, got ready for work, traveled to job, started to work on project or task.

No matter what activities your morning was made up of, take a moment now to identify the breaks between one type of activity and another. (When I say "break," I mean a change from one thing to another, rather than "taking a break.")

Now, image yourself taking a few seconds at the start of each new activity to center yourself within your house of self-love, open to your Greater Self, bring your energy back into your body, ground into the love of the Earth, and focus on being yourself in the upcoming activity.

It sounds like a lot to do, doesn't it? But it really only takes a few seconds, and it feels so good!

Let's try it now. Picture what you are planning to do after reading this chapter. See yourself at the point right before you begin the activity. Now stop and center yourself within your house of self-love. Feel all your Guardians supporting you as you say, "I love myself."

Open to the presence of your Greater Self, and feel it fill you and spread out to fill your house of self-love.

Tune in to your own energy field, and call all your energy back into your body.

Drop energetic roots down into the Earth, and feel love and support flowing up to fill and envelop you.

Focus on the energy of your own heart, and feel your own beautiful "energy signature." Now think of the activity you're about to move into, and move into it in a grounded, centered way, knowing you have the support you need to relax and be yourself throughout the activity.

Having the strong intention to be yourself and staying connected to your heart energy will help you bring forth your own personal magic. You may even be surprised at times by what comes forth from within as you go through your day, taking a few moments before each new activity to center yourself with this practice.

TRUE BELONGING

Now let's talk about bringing authenticity to *all* your relationships—being yourself no matter who you're with.

This is easier said than done, I know, but it's important for us to remember that strong, healthy relationships are built on two people being authentic. Relationships can't be healthy and strong if they're not genuine.

Strong, healthy relationships—just hearing those words can bring to mind the relationships in our lives that are *not* healthy and strong!

Let a few of your relationships come to mind now, and look at them with fresh eyes. Is there one or more that don't feel as good as you'd like?

Take an honest look at what these relationships are based on— are you afraid to be completely yourself? How comfortable are you saying no, voicing your own differing opinions, or admitting your ignorance on topics with which you're unfamiliar?

Think back to when you reflected on a situation in which you felt safe completely being yourself and you thought of a word or phrase that described these feelings.

Bring to mind a relationship in which you have trouble being yourself, and spend a few moments getting clear on the reasons you don't feel safe.

Now connect to the presence of your Guardian Unicorn. Feeling yourself within a field of Unicorn energy, bring your word or phrase to mind and mentally bring it into the energy of this relationship.

Remember that simply becoming aware is a powerful catalyst for transformation, and know that your awareness is bringing a process of positive change to this relationship.

USING THESE IDEAS

I especially like the theme of this chapter, because I love the idea of you showing up as your full, authentic self more of the time!

It's truly refreshing to be around someone who is comfortable being her or himself, and I'm committed to making that our full-time way of being in the world.

Take a few moments now to set some intentions for yourself.

How would you like to use the ideas in this chapter? How do you plan to put some of these ideas into action in order to be yourself more of the time?

It's hard to make huge, lasting changes all at once, so it's okay to ease yourself into this. In which part of your life (or in which relationship) would you like to start?

Once you feel more comfortable with your progress in this area, you can move on to another, becoming more and more true to yourself, and gifting the world with more and more of your radiant, powerful, authentic self.

CHAPTER 17

FREE YOURSELF FROM WORRYING ABOUT WHAT OTHER PEOPLE THINK

Learning to be ourselves brings us face to face with how much we worry about what others think. This can be affecting everything in our lives without our even knowing it!

The first time I encountered the question, "Do you attempt to control how other people see you?" it had a huge impact on me. I don't remember where I read it, just that it was a powerful aha moment, because (a) the answer was a big yes, and (b) I had never thought about it in terms of my trying to *control* something.

We all grow up looking at everyone else's reactions to see how we're doing, because their reactions are powerfully connected to our sense of safety. As adults, much of our sense of safety is *still* tied to other people's opinions of us, trapping us "inside the box"—a box made of other people's opinions.

Freeing ourselves from this trap is vital because when we're focused on worrying about what other people think, we're not thinking for ourselves. We disconnect ourselves from our *own* guidance when we use other people's reactions, opinions, and judgments to define our own self-worth.

So the first step in becoming free from worrying about what other people think is to simply become aware of how much of your energy goes into attempting to control how you're perceived by others.

When I catch myself wanting to control how someone views me, it's kind of a shock to realize how much energy the effort is taking! Check in with yourself. How does this issue apply to you?

Now check in and see how the word *control* feels to you. When we're trying to control how other people think about us, we're doing it from a place of trying to feel safe.

Set an intention to become aware of how much of your energy goes into trying to control how you are perceived by others. Remember to be gentle and supportive of yourself as you observe the power that other people's opinions have in your life.

USE THE SIGNAL OF STRESS TO CONNECT TO YOUR GREATER SELF

I've noticed that often when I'm feeling stressed, that stress is directly related to worrying about what other people think of me. I'm assuming you can relate to this, so it's time to turn your attention to creating a stronger inner foundation by connecting once again to the power of your Greater Self.

As you know, I believe that the person you know yourself to be is a part of a greater eternal being. I call this "whole self" your Greater Self, and even though only a small part of your Greater Self is focused here in physical form, its power and peace is available to you in every moment.

Begin by taking in a nice deep breath. As you exhale, imagine your house of self-love once more around you, and say, "I love myself." Feel the stability of the foundation of this house and the walls around you.

From within this house of self-love, feel yourself fully in your body, with all your consciousness and energy centered within your physical form.

Now open yourself to the presence of your Greater Self. Feel this connection in your heart, and as you do, notice what else you feel in your body.

Ground yourself down into the Earth, and feel it supporting you in staying aware of your Greater Self.

As you go through your day, notice when you are feeling stress, and consider it a signal. Check in to see if that stress is connected to worrying about someone else's opinion of you.

If it is, take a moment to invoke your house of self-love, get fully back in your body, and feel the presence and power of your Greater Self.

EXAMINE YOUR MOTIVATIONS

Worrying about what other people think is a trap that affects all of us to some extent, because it's intertwined with our sense of self-worth, and that in turn is tied to our need to be safe.

The feelings we're afraid of usually come from past experiences of being ridiculed or criticized or feeling we didn't fit in. We end up believing we're not good enough somehow, and these feelings are so painful that we try to push them down. In doing so we end up *integrating* them into all our motives.

In this way, other people's opinions can become a guiding force in our lives, without our even being aware of it. So set an intention to become aware of the underlying motivations for your actions and your plans. Become aware of the situations in your life where you are focused on an end result of other's people's positive judgment.

If you find that, at its heart, your motivation for a particular action is focused on someone else's good opinion of you, you can choose to stop and turn within.

Connect to your Greater Self, check in with your own inner guidance, and empower yourself in that moment to be the only judge of what's right, worthy, appropriate, acceptable, and valuable for *you.*

IDENTIFY THE RULE BOOK IN YOUR HEAD

The next step is to become aware of all of the "shoulds" you carry around inside your head and reassess the rules you've internalized about the "right" way to be.

Set an intention now to get clear about the places in your life where you're trying to conform to an outside set of standards about the "way things are done" or "the right way to do things."

This may take some internal digging, but it's worth it, because when we catch ourselves trying to conform in order to be accepted, it's a signal that we're not feeling worthy and empowered.

Begin to notice the places where you're not motivated by love for whatever you're doing, but instead are trying to prove your worth and acceptability by conforming to an external set of standards.

When you catch yourself, make a mental note or use your journal to record the thoughts and feelings that are coming up, and get to the heart of what your *true* intentions are.

The problem with carrying around outside standards and rule books in our heads is that since they're not coming from inside, they're not necessarily in alignment with our own divine guidance, which lets us know *in every moment* what's right for us.

When we live our lives according to outside rules and standards, we cut ourselves off from true happiness and fulfillment, because we can only really be satisfied when we're fulfilling the true desires that come from within us.

So identify the rule book in your head and reassess it, using your own powerful inner wisdom.

Give yourself the power to decide what *you* feel is the right way to do things, based on your own inner guidance. You may find that you end up doing a lot of the very same things, but you'll be doing them from an empowered place of love and choice, rather than from a need to feel good enough.

I'm sending you love as you begin to live from the light of your own heart!

EXAMINE THE ISSUE OF CONFORMITY

Needing to conform is an underlying, foundational part of our unconscious worry about what others think.

Everyone in every society is conditioned to focus on what other people think to some degree. It's one of the ways societies keep us in line, and it affects all of us.

So when you become more attuned to what's inside you and begin to break out of the mold of conformity to be original—in whatever way that shows up for you—some people will be comfortable with it (and even welcome it), and some people will disapprove.

People will be comfortable with your nonconformity to the extent that they are comfortable with the idea of nonconformity itself.

Some people are very comfortable marching to the beat of their own drum, and other people are only comfortable when they're living in accordance with a larger set of rules and a group that lives by those same rules.

To live authentically, we need to get clear on what feels right to us based on our *own* system of beliefs, instead of just conforming in order to feel safe.

Each one of us has a powerful inner guidance system that points us toward the right thing for us in every moment, and a habit of conformity gets in the way of that guidance.

If this resonates with you, begin noticing when the issue of conformity raises its head in your life. See it for what it is, and decide for yourself if conforming really does keep you safe.

Bringing the subject into the light of your awareness will strengthen and empower you in wonderful ways.

REASSESS THE VALUE OF APPROVAL

What is the actual value of receiving outside approval? What do you need it for? This is not a rhetorical question. Get clear now on the *purpose* approval serves in your life and how you feel it supports you.

Take a deep breath, let it out slowly, and ground yourself into the love of the Earth. Feel the walls of your house of self-love around you, and connect to the power and wisdom of your Greater Self.

Think about the times in your life when you've had outside approval for who you are and what you are doing, and also think about the times when you didn't have that outside approval.

Now ask yourself: "What is the actual value of that approval to you?"

It's an interesting question, isn't it?

Of course, getting approval feels so good! But disapproval feels awful, and when we seek one, we're often stuck with the other.

Instead of just fighting against disapproval, it helps to recognize that disapproval doesn't actually have the power to hurt you, and approval doesn't have the power to keep you safe.

Play around with the idea of seeing both approval and disapproval as valueless. They are just two sides of a meaningless coin.

TAKE OWNERSHIP OF YOUR OWN SELF-WORTH

As you go through the days ahead, observe your own reactions to what other people think, and sit with those feelings. Then commit yourself to taking ownership of your own self-worth.

This way you can begin to love the people in your life on a deeper level, because it's impossible to *truly* love them while you're giving them authority over you.

Freeing yourself from what other people think of you will make your essence shine brighter in the world, and your presence will become more and more a blessing and a gift.

Once we stop defining our self-worth by other people's judgments, we can begin fulfilling ourselves by actually filling our lives with what we love.

Take ownership of your own self-worth now, and base it on expressing what you love.

CHAPTER 18

FORGIVE IN A NEW WAY WITH THE UNICORNS

When we're frustrated in creating what we want in our lives, sometimes it's because there's a negative energy pattern in the way. To put it another way, there may be something we need to forgive.

Many spiritual teachings cite forgiveness as a key to life, but they don't really show us *how* to forgive.

So we talk a lot about forgiveness, and we try to use the love in our hearts in order to forgive, but many times our attempts at forgiveness are frustrating and disappointing. More often than not, we find ourselves still holding on to negative feelings toward the one we're trying to forgive.

Over the years, I've seen many well-meaning people talk about how they *completely* forgive those who have hurt them. But I've seen these same people experience more and more pain and illness in their bodies with each year that passes.

When you try to put the "correct" feelings on top of how you really feel, it may feel like you're achieving something, but your unresolved emotions and pain are actually just muddying up your energy field—and getting pushed into your body.

The ability to forgive *is* an important key in our lives. But we need to think of forgiveness in a new way.

151

RECLAIMING YOUR ENERGY

Even though the things we need to forgive may have happened in the past, the energies they created are active within us in the present. When your energy is locked into a negative pattern, you may feel an emotional charge every time you think of a certain person or situation.

Whenever you think of someone or something and the thought brings with it a bad feeling, it shows you that part of your energy is locked up in an active, harmful thought pattern. It's important to pay attention to these signals and take action to transform your energy.

In this chapter we'll reclaim our energy from old painful patterns. We'll use a systematic approach, and we'll call on the power and grace of the Unicorns to assist us in reclaiming, purifying, and uplifting our energy fields.

This kind of forgiveness is a process of pulling your energy out of negative patterns. Until you forgive—by which I mean reclaim your energy—a vital part of your energy will be locked up, vibrating in a negative way.

Like everything in this book, forgiveness is a skill we can learn.

OBSTACLES TO FORGIVENESS

Before we learn a new way to forgive, it's important to talk about the obstacles to forgiving. The first obstacle most of us face is not knowing *how* to truly accomplish forgiveness.

The solution to this problem is to think of forgiveness in energetic terms. Remember, the situation you need to forgive created a painful energy pattern that you carry within you.

This is important to recognize, because negative energy patterns affect everything you attempt to create in the present. They are part of your current energetic makeup, even if the event that caused them happened many years in the past.

When you look at forgiveness in this way, you'll see that it's really just a process of *pulling your energy out of an old pattern*. This automatically empowers you and restores a big chunk of your personal energy.

The next thing that makes forgiveness so hard is that we don't want to let the guilty party off the hook for what they did.

The painful events we've experienced in our lives have negatively affected the way we feel about ourselves. These events may have made us feel undeserving or unworthy.

Or we may feel robbed of the time we devoted in a failed relationship, and it feels like that time can never be given back to us.

Without realizing it, we may feel that the thing that was done to us or the situation we experienced has changed our life in a fundamental way, limiting our future potential.

Try this right now: focus on the idea of forgiveness, and let someone pop into your mind.

Look into your heart and see if you've got a core belief that this person changed what's possible for you to have.

Now go a step further. Look within yourself and see if the bad experience you had with this person has also changed your behavior. How were you different before this person negatively affected your life? (This applies even if the person was a parent. Imagine yourself at the moment of your birth, and connect to the beautiful, shining core qualities you possessed.)

There is nothing that can possibly happen in our lives that has more power than the Source power that's running through us. That universal power can't be affected by anything physical that happens.

This awareness is a vital key to forgiveness.

When we are profoundly wounded as children (or at any time in our lives), it can leave us feeling damaged, as if something fundamental within us is broken. It can feel as if something vital was taken from us, and so we may have a stubborn desire to have that something fixed or given back to us by the person who did the damage.

If there is someone in your past who hurt you so profoundly that you need them to change what they did, then you're not allowing yourself to move forward and be happy without *that person* fixing what they did to your self-esteem.

But if you are willing to move forward and let the *Universe* compensate you for everything that's happened in your past, and if you are willing to be happy and to feel good, no matter what happened, then your life can continue to become better and better, regardless of what happened in your past.

From now on, be willing to release that old locked-up energy. Let the power of Source energy restore and repair everything within you that is damaged.

Let go of the need for compensation from the person who wronged you, and let the Unicorns assist you in reclaiming and purifying your energy.

The willingness to be happy and to be compensated for everything that's happened—not from the person who did it, but from the Universe—is the willingness you need in order to live the life you are meant to live.

OUR FORGIVENESS PROCEDURE

When I set about to create my own version of a forgiveness process, I was inspired by the forgiveness teachings of Catherine Ponder and Carole Doré.

The forgiveness procedure I use has two parts: the words you say and the energy you create.

The words alone won't accomplish anything, but the words give you a way to organize your thoughts and your own energetic power. They give you a way to tap into the force that will create lasting positive change in your life.

The most important factor in the forgiveness process is to connect to Source energy, and the Unicorns can assist you with this.

Let's go through it together. We'll pretend that I'm forgiving a woman named Mary Jones. I start by stating my name:

"I am Kim.

"I am fully connected to the Source power within me.

"I call on the Unicorns to support me and love me.

"I choose to forgive Mary Jones completely, and now I am free.

"I bless her with Source love and light and release her to her highest good, and the Source power within her blesses me with Source love and light, and releases me to my highest good.

"The love and light of the Unicorns raises us both to new patterns of love and happiness.

"I receive a wealth of goodness from the situation, and I step forward into a new level of love, happiness, and fulfillment."

Those are the words, but on their own, the words won't do much for you. So let's go through the process, and I'll show you what to do as you say those words.

To begin, state who you are: *"I am . . ."* This brings you back into your own energy. We spend all day looking at everyone else and picking up their energy, emotions, and vibrations, so begin this process by getting back into your own self.

After you state your first name, then drop a grounding cord into the Earth and feel yourself grounded and supported by the Earth's love. Get a sense of your own energy boundary, an arm's length around you in all directions.

Then say the second part: *"I am fully connected to the Source power within me."* You can substitute another word for *Source*, but I strongly suggest that you include the word *power*.

Some people want to substitute the word *love* for the word *power* because they're uncomfortable with the idea of power. This can be because they've had painful experiences in the past where they were overpowered or where someone's power was used against them.

The reason it's so important to use the word *power* is that it reconnects you to the fact that Source power supersedes anything in the physical world. This power is 100 percent love. Our idea of love is much more limited than this power.

Next, you say: *"I call on the Unicorns to support me and love me."* Feel them on either side of you or all around you. Picture them alongside the person you are forgiving as well.

"I choose to forgive (person's name) completely, and now I am free. I bless her (or whatever pronouns they use) with Source love and light and release her to her highest good, and the Source power within her blesses me with source love and light, and releases me to my highest good." This is an important step, feeling that the higher self of the other person is also releasing you.

"The love and light of the Unicorns raises us both to new patterns of love and happiness. I receive a wealth of goodness from the situation, and I step forward into a new level of love, happiness, and fulfillment." As you finish with these lines, really feel this in every part of your being. Then thank Source, thank the Unicorns, and ground down into the Earth's embrace once more.

Get comfortable with the words in the forgiveness procedure (as well as the energy *within* the words).

APPLYING FORGIVENESS

Now let's apply the forgiveness procedure to the places in our lives that need it most. We'll tap into the power of the sacred space we create here together to hold us as we free ourselves more and more through the power of forgiveness, relying on our own wisdom to bring to our minds the people we most need to forgive.

Take a nice deep breath, ask Angels to be in the four corners of the room you are in, and ground down into the Earth's love.

Take a moment to let a person you need to forgive come into your mind.

Now do the procedure along with me. I'll leave space for you to say your and the other person's name and their pronouns.

"I am (your name).

"I am fully connected to the Source power within me.

"I call on the Unicorns to support me and love me.

"I choose to forgive (person's name) completely, and now I am free.

"I bless (person's name) with Source love and light and release (them) to (their) highest good, and the Source power within (them) blesses me with Source love and light, and releases me to my highest good.

"The love and light of the Unicorns raises us both to new patterns of love and happiness.

"I receive a wealth of goodness from the situation, and I step forward into a new level of love, happiness, and fulfillment."

Take a moment to check in and notice how you feel now. What do you feel in your body?

Now let's do it again, for the same person.

"I am (your name).

"I am fully connected to the Source power within me.

"I call on the Unicorns to support me and love me.

"I choose to forgive (person's name) completely, and now I am free.

"I bless (person's name) with Source love and light and release (them) to (their) highest good, and the Source power within (them) blesses me with Source love and light, and releases me to my highest good.

"The love and light of the Unicorns raises us all to new patterns of love and happiness.

"I receive a wealth of goodness from the situation, and I step forward into a new level of love, happiness, and fulfillment."

Check in with your body again.

Take a moment now to thank the Angels and the Unicorns.

Any time the person you are forgiving comes into your mind today, repeat the process, noticing each time how you feel before and after the procedure.

UNBURDENING YOURSELF FIRST

I was once going through a rough patch in my relationship with a family member. The relationship was a mix of good and bad, but I found myself unable to focus on the good things he did, because I was chronically annoyed by all the things that irritated me! Over and over again, I spent my time with him feeling annoyed.

I finally realized I needed to transform my energy around this person with the forgiveness procedure. But when I began, I felt myself unwilling to actually start the procedure, because my many little resentments were just throbbing away, front and center.

I felt my Guardian Unicorns at my side, and I became aware of their energy creating a sparkling rainbow energy field in front of me.

In my mind, I began speaking my resentments as if I were venting to an understanding friend. One by one, I spoke my feelings into the sparkling space in front of me. And as I did, I felt each one leave me.

One particularly yucky judgmental thought felt lodged in my solar plexus. I imagined my own hand moving into the energetic space there and pushing the energy of this thought out of my body and into the Unicorn energy, severing its connection with me.

After a few minutes of this, I noticed myself speaking my own regrets into the field of sparkling energy. "I feel bad about the time I . . ." and so on.

Before long, I felt ready and willing to do the actual forgiveness procedure. You can try the unburdening process yourself with the following exercise:

> Connect to the presence of the Guardian Unicorns at your sides. Close your eyes and see their energy filling the space before you.

> Mentally speak your feelings and resentments into this space of Unicorn energy. Unburden yourself of all your negative feelings about this person, one by one.

> You may find there are many layers of stuck energy, so you may choose to do this over and over. Each time you do it, you're freeing up and reclaiming more and more of your energy.

FORGIVING YOURSELF

We can't talk about the subject of forgiving others without thinking about the times we need to forgive ourselves. If there's something you haven't been able to forgive in yourself, start by using the unburdening process we just discussed. Then move on to our self-forgiveness procedure.

In this example, I need to forgive myself for something I did to "John."

"I am Kim.

"I am fully connected to the Source power within me.

"I call on the Unicorns to support me and love me.

"I choose to forgive myself completely for _____, and now John and I are both free.

"I bring my past thoughts and actions to Source love and light and release them to be transformed into the highest good, and the Source power within John blesses him with Source love and light, and uplifts him to his highest good.

"The love and light of the Unicorns purifies my thoughts, my actions, and everything within me.

"John receives a wealth of goodness from the situation, and we both step forward into a new level of love, happiness, and expansion."

Now try the following self-forgiveness procedure:

With the Unicorns at your sides, speak your regret or guilt into the field of Unicorn energy.

"I am (your name).

"I am fully connected to the Source power within me.

"I call on the Unicorns to support me and love me.

"I choose to forgive myself completely for _____, and now we are both free.

"*I bring my thoughts and actions to Source love and light and release them to be transformed into the highest good, and the Source power within (name of person you feel you have wronged) blesses (them) with Source love and light, and uplifts (them) to (their) highest good.*

"*The love and light of the Unicorns purifies my thoughts, actions, and everything within me.*

"*(Person's name) receives a wealth of goodness from the situation, and we both step forward into a new level of love, happiness, and expansion.*"

You might choose to make the forgiveness procedure a regular part of your morning practice, allowing the thought of people you need to forgive to come into your mind and then freeing up your energy with the procedure.

Keep this procedure in your personal toolkit and use it often. I can't wait to see what you create with your reclaimed energy and power!

CHAPTER 19

TELL YOURSELF A NEW STORY

All day, every day, we talk to ourselves, telling ourselves stories about the meaning of events in our past and the meaning behind what's happening in our lives right now. Your current life is a direct reflection of the stories you hold in your heart and mind—the stories you tell yourself over and over.

These stories reflect the "truths" that shape our lives. I put quotes around the word *truths* because our stories are *not* really true, but we hold them in our hearts and live from them anyway, without even being aware that we're doing it.

In this chapter you'll become more and more aware of the stories you are telling yourself. You'll empower yourself to tell new stories based on what's really true—true about who and what you are, and true about what's possible for you.

Our stories are made up of the conclusions we've drawn from everything that's happened in our lives, and these conclusions—the *meaning* we take from events—often cause us more pain than the events themselves.

So often we take away a disempowering meaning—a meaning that affects the way we feel about ourselves and about what's possible for us in life. As we continue to tell ourselves a disempowering story, the story shapes our view of how the world works, and even more importantly, it shapes our beliefs about our place in the world.

Our stories run continually below the surface, affecting everything we think and do.

The stories you tell yourself are like computer programs running in the background, twenty-four hours a day. They have nothing to do with who you truly are and what's truly possible for you to create.

But they do have the power to limit what you *believe* is possible. More than anything, the negative stories we tell ourselves are limiting. Our stories define the limits of the lives we're creating for ourselves.

Let's take away these false limits now. The limiting things you believe about yourself (based on the meaning you've taken away from painful events) are not true.

They are not based on the authentic truth of your being.

Let's focus now on releasing the limiting stories you carry in your heart, so you can move forward freely and create a life that fully represents who you are and what you love.

OUR STORIES ARE BUILDING BLOCKS

It's time to become more aware of the stories we tell ourselves. This is important, because our stories are the building blocks with which we create our lives. If you've got a preponderance of negative stories running in your mind, you're trying to create an amazing life using second-rate building blocks.

Many of the stories we tell ourselves are based on distorted mirrors—things reflected back to us by others that caused us to believe something negative about ourselves.

Every time you've experienced something painful, you've internalized a "meaning" from the experience, and the bigger the painful event, the deeper the meaning you are holding in your heart.

Every meaning you take away from painful events gets added to your own "internal database" about how life works, about who you are, and about what you should expect in the future.

Situations that scared you may have created an internal story that life is dangerous, and the things you've experienced that made you feel not good enough have created ongoing stories based on that "fact."

If we don't achieve a goal, we usually take away the meaning that we were not good enough to achieve that goal. We carry that belief with us, and it gathers momentum. We gather more and more beliefs that are like it, and those beliefs become the building blocks with which we build our lives.

But these disempowering stories, just like subpar building blocks, can be discarded. You can replace them with life-enriching stories that reflect the real truth of your being.

Let's stop and do this now. Take in a nice, fresh deep breath, ground yourself into the love of the Earth, and clear your mind.

Now let something, anything, come into your mind.

Was the thing that came into your mind something that makes you feel good or not so good?

If the thing that came into your mind—whatever it is—is something that makes you feel good, then you know that the story you're holding in your heart about that thing is a helpful story, something that's empowering and supporting you.

If you got a bad feeling about what came into your mind, you know that the program running—the story you chronically tell yourself about that issue—is an unhelpful story.

It's a story that is not reflecting the whole truth. It is not reflecting the truth of your beauty and value, and/or it's not reflecting the truth of how life works and what's truly possible for you.

You can create a new story for yourself around this issue, one that encourages, supports, and empowers you to live your heart's desires.

BRING ONE OF YOUR STORIES INTO THE LIGHT OF YOUR AWARENESS

Let's bring one of your stories into the full light of your awareness now, so you can assess its value as a building block in your life.

Let's start by bringing to mind a painful event from your past. (Not so major that it brings you to your knees to think about it, but significant enough that you know you're still carrying "baggage" from it.)

Think of the painful event, and tune in to the story you took away from it.

I'll guide you through some prompts, and you can fill in the blanks in your journal or say or think them as part of this exercise.

What happened was _____.

As a result, I feel that I _____.

The story I tell myself is that it's not safe to _____ because I'm _____.

Focusing on this story can be really liberating or really heavy (or a combination of both!), so be gentle with yourself right now.

Center yourself within your house of self-love and say, "I love myself." Open to the presence of your Greater Self, and take a few moments to feel it fill you and spread out all around you.

Tune in to your own energy field, and call all your energy back into your body. Drop energetic roots down into the Earth, and feel love and support and nourishment flowing up to you.

Call on your Guardian Unicorns to help you know yourself truly, and feel their presence on either side of you.

Stay connected to your Guardian Unicorns as you continue to allow all the parts and versions of this story to come into your awareness. Rather than seeing this story as something inside you, see it as something spread out before you now.

In a moment, we'll begin the process of transforming this story, but take a moment now to remember that you are safe and supported, and that I am sending you love as you bring this story out of yourself and into the light.

TRANSFORMING YOUR STORY

With the last exercise, you did the important work of bringing one of your stories into the light of your awareness.

Now we'll allow this story to be transformed into a building block that will serve you as you create the life you are meant to live.

Feel the presence of Angels in the four corners of the room or space you're in, and let their energy fill you and uplift you.

Center yourself within your house of self-love and say, "I love myself." Open to the presence of your Greater Self, and feel it fill you and spread out all around you.

Tune in to your own energy field, and call all your energy back into your body. Drop energetic roots down into the Earth, and feel love, support, and new life flowing up to fill you.

Remember the presence of your Guardian Unicorns. With your Unicorn Guardians at your side, go deeper within, until you find yourself standing in a small clearing in a forest. This forest is filled with love and magic, and everything glows with uplifting energy.

In the center of the clearing lies a toppled-down Tree. This Tree looks very, very old, and as you get closer you somehow know that this Tree was hit by lightning.

This lightning-struck Tree is filled with even more magic than the rest of this forest, and there is a hollowed-out space in its trunk that calls to you now.

As you stand before this Tree, reach inside yourself and collect all the parts and pieces of your old story. Gather up the energy of this old story, and move it outside of you now.

Place the energy of this story into the hollowed-out space in the ancient Tree before you.

Watch as sparkling pink energy rises, almost like fireflies, up from the Tree to envelop your story.

The energy of your outgrown story grows fainter and fainter, until all that's left is a pale pink glow.

Now, with the Tree and your Guardian Unicorns supporting you, tell your new, updated story. You can write this in your journal or say or think it as part of this exercise.

"What happened was _____," and this time as you tell the story, remember that you are beautiful and valuable, and that you are meant to be happy.

Tap into the support of this magical place as you retell your story: "Because this happened, I feel _____."

Finally, connect to your own inner power and the power of change held within the lightning-struck Tree. "Because this happened, I can now _____."

Come all the way back to your normal waking state, holding this magical place within you.

SCARY STORIES

As you practice telling yourself new stories, pay attention to the words you use in conversations and see if any of them have their roots in a disempowering story you've been telling yourself.

Look into the *core* of your stories, and see if any common themes emerge. You might even want to use your journal to name each one of your stories. Next to each story's title, write down its major theme or message.

You may find that certain themes or messages are repeated over and over.

Seeing this is a breakthrough, because you're the one creating your life, and you have all the power you need to change your own personal patterns by creating new personal stories.

Take a deep breath now, and if you're in a safe space, think of something you are worried about.

Take a few moments to identify the scary story you are telling yourself about this issue.

Now create a new story.

Start like this: "I am (your name). I am fully connected to Source, fully connected to the love of the Earth, and fully connected to my Greater Self.

"I came into this world to fulfill my personal divine mission, and I have everything I need to express my full potential.

"I can count on my Guardians to help and support me every step of the way as I create a beautiful, powerful life."

Now think of how you would love to see this situation unfold. Take a few moments to visualize it like a film in your mind.

Allow this to be the new story you tell yourself. Whenever you catch yourself worrying, repeat this process!

STORIES ABOUT YOUR LOVED ONES

It's time to bring our focus to the scary stories we tell ourselves about the people we love.

I have two kids, and even though they're both grown adults, I still catch myself worrying about them. So let's use a formula for creating new, positive stories about the people we love.

Fill in the blanks for the story you're currently telling yourself:

"I worry that (a situation or behavior) will cause (bad thing you're afraid of) to happen to (loved one's name)."

Now apply the new-story statement we just used.

"I am (your name). I know that (loved one's name) is connected to Source, is receiving love from the Earth, and has an unbreakable connection to (their) Greater Self.

"(Person's name) came into this world to fulfill (their) personal divine mission, and (they) have everything (they) need to express (their) full potential. I know (they) have Guardian Beings to help and support (them) every step of the way as (they) create a beautiful, powerful life."

Now fill in the following blanks to create a new story:

"(Person's name) is learning, growing wiser and stronger, and gaining valuable life experience from (situation). I see (her) life getting better with every year that passes, and I see (her) feeling more and more fulfilled."

Notice how your own energy feels as you do this, and feel yourself becoming more and more aligned with positive outcomes.

A STURDY NEW BUILDING BLOCK

The work you've done here to transform the stories you tell yourself is something you can return to again and again, as needed. We'll end with a focus on something you want to create.

Think of something you'd love to create in your life, something you're not currently experiencing. Now think of an imaginary person who is already experiencing the thing you want to create.

Spend a few moments imagining the story that she must have told herself in order to align with this outcome. At first you may just think of random thoughts and ideas. Collect these, and use them to create a new story.

Keep bringing your attention back to this exercise until you have created an inspiring, empowering story for yourself. Then stay conscious of this story, repeating it to yourself as often as possible.

May this story become a sturdy, stable building block, and may you create many more like it as you consciously create the life that's right for you

CHAPTER 20

∽୨୧∽

RECLAIM YOUR SPARK

I'm going to start this chapter by asking you a question: What sparks you?

The things that spark a fire within you—your personal passions—are so important because they are the keys to claiming your spiritual gifts and fulfilling your soul purpose.

Check in now: Are your personal passions an integral part of your life? Or do you think of them as luxuries—something you don't have the time or money to pursue?

Passion is an interesting word, and it has different meanings, but my definition is "a compelling love."

The word *compelling* is key here, because our passions move us to *do or express* something that will connect us with whatever it is that we love.

This chapter is about discovering and liberating your passions. Each one is a personal map that will guide you on your life's journey and show you how to share the countless gifts you have brought with you into the world.

BRIGID'S FIRE

As we create an inner Gateway to access the energy of passion, the perfect Guardian to call on for support is the Goddess Brigid.

Brigid is a Celtic Goddess of healing, poetry, inspiration, and the transforming fire of the forge and Earth. The fire within her brings the spark of life to everything she touches, and she can help you reclaim and tend the fire within your own heart.

Close your eyes, ground yourself into the love of the Earth, and go within yourself to the sacred place that connects you to the Great Mother.

Within this sacred place, Brigid appears before you, radiant in her green cloak. In her presence you feel a powerful sense of peace and safety, and within this energy of safety, you feel the spark of your own inner fire.

Brigid reaches out and places her hand on your heart, and you feel her love feeding the flames of your inner fire.

All the events and experiences that have served to dampen your inner fire are burned away now in the light of her sacred flame.

Allow yourself to feel all your cells awakening now, nourished by the sparks of your own passions. As you open your eyes and return to your normal waking state, feel the new life in every part of your body.

Thank Brigid and continue to feel her steady hand on your heart as you go through your day. Everything that has been blocking you is now falling away, and the path before you is opening up, lit by the fire within your own heart.

Feel the love and support in the space we share, and own the power of your own inner fire today.

WHAT DOES IT MEAN TO RECLAIM YOUR SPARK?

At the beginning of this chapter, I asked you to think of what sparks you, and now I'm going to ask again.

What wakes you up? What excites you? What stimulates you?

Your passions are the maps to your soul purpose *and* the engine that moves you down the path of that purpose.

The spark we're reclaiming is energy, in a raw, potent form.

Along with feeling unfulfilled, when we're not living according to our own soul purpose, we also can have a nameless sense of dread.

This can show up as anxiety or depression or the "just not right" feeling that comes whenever we're not living according to our own unique divine blueprint.

So once again, ask yourself the question, "What sparks me?"

One thing that sparks me is creativity in all its different forms. I love to engage in the act of creating something from nothing or creating something new from something old.

I'm even excited when I watch a TV show or movie about someone who is fully expressing *their* creativity.

Take a moment now and think about the things that enliven you.

Make a rough list in your mind or in your journal as ideas begin to come to you.

Passions are different than regular loves. There are lots and lots of things we love, but passions make us feel alive in a way nothing else can.

When you consciously connect with the things that spark you, you tap into an internal power source. You get a jolt of pure life-force energy that awakens you, enlivens you, and makes you want to take action.

RECOGNIZE THE IMPORTANCE OF YOUR PASSIONS

When you think about the things you love, you'll find a few core things that you'll recognize as your passions. Connecting to these passions will fill you with fresh life-force energy and strengthen you from the inside out.

Bring to mind three of your personal passions.

For each one, think of a number on a scale of 1 through 10 that represents how much you're currently connecting to that passion.

For example, three of the things on my own list are creativity, movies and TV, and travel. Remember, these aren't just things that I love, they are things that excite me, wake me up, and make me want to take action.

I'm currently engaged in expressing a lot of creativity in my work and in my home, so I think on a scale of 1 through 10, with 1 being the least and 10 being the most, I would choose the numbers 8 or 9 to reflect how much I'm channeling my love of creativity.

Now on to TV and movies. I don't just like to watch TV and films, I'm very sparked by the way they are made. I spent a couple of days on the set of an independent film a few years ago, and I can't begin to tell you how much the process enlivened me. But I've been so busy with my work that it's something I haven't been thinking about much, so I think I'd have to give it a 1 or 2 rating right now.

Travel is something I tend to put off for another time when life gets busy, but I do have a trip planned in the next couple of months, so I'll rate it at 3.

Take a few more moments to rate how much you are currently connecting to another three of your own passions.

How do you feel after looking at your relationship with your passions this way?

Making a list like this makes us realize that even though *thinking* about our passions excites us, what keeps us connected to the energizing life force of our passions is *taking action* to express them.

And that brings us to one of the reasons we lose our spark in the first place: it's not always easy to take action on our passions!

If you're finding that you're not connected *at all* to your passions, don't worry. As with everything, becoming aware is the step that changes everything.

Remember, you have your passions for a reason—they fuel you as you move on the path that's right for you. Even if your true passions have been ignored for years, they still exist within you, and you can fan them back into flames with the right kind of attention.

For now, be gentle with yourself, and celebrate the fact that you are learning how to bring fresh, joy-filled energy into your being and into your life.

CONNECT TO YOUR PASSIONS EVERY DAY

As we move through this chapter together, you're accessing the living energy field of passion and reclaiming your spark—connecting more and more to the things that make you feel fired up and fully alive.

You don't have to wait for something outside you to bring you this feeling. Creating consistent daily time to connect with your passions is a powerful thing you can begin to do for yourself.

As I've said, your passions connect you to your life force in a way nothing else can, so when you're connected to your passions, you'll feel a flow of energy coming into you.

But passions are also something that you feed—it's a reciprocal system. One of the ways you can begin to feed your passions is by changing the way you look at them, putting them in a place of importance, and thinking of them in a *sacred* way.

Knowing that your passions are sacred and creating a daily ritual of connecting with the things you love will help keep each one from becoming just another thing on your to-do list.

Take a nice deep breath, and as you exhale, allow yourself to relax. Feel the warm energy of the Goddess Brigid all around you. Feel her hand on your heart, and allow yourself to relax into a wonderful feeling of safety and love.

Now bring to mind three things that spark you. Allow yourself a few moments of daydreaming about the first one. Keep it lighthearted and playful, and make sure it feels good.

Now let yourself daydream about the second one. Remember to keep it lighthearted and playful.

And now let yourself daydream about your third passion.

From now on, make this a fun daily ritual. Recognize your passions as a powerful part of who you are meant to be, and know that as you feed them, they will feed you.

BOOK OF PASSIONS

As we recognize the importance of our personal passions and begin to feed them with our love and attention, their presence within us grows bright enough to light our way. You can support this process by creating something physical to help you explore and deepen your connection to what sparks you.

If this idea appeals to you, consider creating your own "Book of Passions." This can be done in any form you like. You might use a notebook, binder, or journal. (I recommend that your Book of Passions be physical, if possible, and not digital.)

Begin using this book as a sacred, fertile place to store and record everything that sparks you in both small and large ways. These could take the form of pictures you paste in, quotes you copy down, or random thoughts and inspirations you record in writing.

Try not to overthink this process. Our intention is to make this a space to step outside of linear thinking, so compile all the things your heart cries out for—even if they make no logical sense.

You can also use your imagination to create an energetic Book of Passions to go alongside your physical book. As you go through your days, start calling out to the things that will spark you, and when they show up, mentally record them in your energetic or physical Book of Passions.

Keep this book and your passions alive in your heart!

YOUR INNER GARDEN

We'll end this chapter with a journey to your own magical inner garden.

Close your eyes, take a nice deep breath, relax as you exhale, and go within until you find yourself in a lush garden. This garden is filled with beautiful plants and flowers that represent the different aspects of your own being.

Walk around and take in the beauty you see all around you. It's a special beauty, because it's filled with your own unique energy, and as you walk around this garden, you feel perfectly in sync with everything you see.

The Goddess Brigid is with you here, supporting you with every one of your creations, and you thank her for her presence. As you connect with the gorgeous flowers in this garden, you notice beautiful fruit Trees spreading their branches above you. These Trees represent your passions, and as you give each one your love, you see its fruit growing more plentiful.

Walk closer to one of these Trees, and identify the passion it represents. Feel yourself at one with this grand, sturdy Tree, and thank it for its presence within your being. Reach up and pluck one of its fruits, and watch as the fruit transforms into a gift for you.

Bring this gift back with you as you open your eyes.

As you go through today and the days to come, stay conscious of the gift you've received, and know there are many more waiting for you.

Reclaim your spark, fan it into flames, and let the glow of this inner fire light your way from now on.

CHAPTER 21

‿✎‿

FOCUS ON WHAT YOU WANT

As you know, one of my favorite Abraham-Hicks teachings states that when you experience something you don't want, something new is created in energetic form. This new creation is the opposite of that unwanted experience—it's something better that matches who you're *truly* meant to be.

In this way, you grow as a creator, and life continues to expand.

The problem is, we tend to keep focusing on the things we Don't Want, and so the energy of the things we Don't Want stays active within us.

We're going to create a breakthrough for ourselves now by attuning ourselves to the situations and experiences that match the love in our hearts. We'll do it by focusing on what we *Do* Want.

(I like to think of Do Want and Don't Want with capital letters, because it helps me see them as choices!)

We're all used to focusing on things we Don't Want. It's a habit. We tend to be problem-oriented because we think that's the way to create a solution.

But it actually just creates more of what we Don't Want.

Once you get in the habit of focusing on what you really Do Want, you'll begin to see big payoffs, but it takes a willingness to look at the way you're thinking and feeling on a habitual, ongoing basis.

All the work you've done in this book will be undone if you continue to focus on what you Don't Want.

So in this chapter we'll take advantage of a common three-step Law of Attraction process to focus on what we Do Want, looking at the important parts of our lives one by one.

I'm betting you are already familiar with this process, but I'm *also* betting you're not using it all the time! It's time to change that, with the help of your Guardian Angel and the Spirit of the Earth.

Step One is to focus on a part of your life and let what you Don't Want come into your awareness. What you Don't Want might be a current experience, or it might be something you're afraid of. Either way, let it come into your mind.

Next, open your mind to allow in a different way of looking at the existence of what you Don't Want. Instead of thinking of its presence as proof that something has gone wrong, recognize that its presence is *proof* that its opposite is available for you to experience.

Step Two is the hard part: think of what you *Do* Want in this situation. This shouldn't be hard, but it is, because we're so negatively attached to the things we Don't Want!

Really commit yourself to this process and focus on determining what it is you Do Want in this instance.

Step Three is to attune yourself to the energy of what you Do Want. Do this not with the intention of trying to force it to happen, but instead with the intention to create and carry beautiful energy within you that matches the things you love. Let's try it now with the subject of your body.

Let any Don't Wants come into your mind, and thank them for directing you to their opposites.

Focus on the energy in your heart, and feel the presence of your Guardian Angel there. Connect to the power of the beautiful pattern of energy it holds for you concerning your body.

Supported by your Guardian Angel, spend a few moments deciding what you Do Want for your body. (You can choose just one aspect of your body to focus on if it makes it easier.)

Let yourself playfully think about why you want the things you Do Want for your body. Do this in a light way, focusing on how you love to feel certain ways or how you love to be able to do certain things. Do this from your heart, and keep doing it until you notice that your heart is feeling full and happy.

From this full and happy place, imagine a little scene in which you're living what you Do Want for your body.

This brings you into communion with the living energy of the state you are desiring. For example, if you're holding happy, joyful thoughts about health, you're creating a Gateway in your heart that connects you to the living energy field of health.

Sense the presence of this Gateway to health within you now, and let yourself become one with this vibrant, living energy. Absorb the energy of health into every part of your body, and thank it with love.

When you're done, ground yourself into the love of the Earth and notice what you feel in your body now.

In the remainder of this chapter, we'll apply this process to several major parts of your life. Once you have done the work of choosing what you Do Want in each situation, you won't have to start from scratch each time, and getting back in alignment with what you'd love will be much easier.

FOCUS ON WHAT YOU **WANT** FOR YOUR HOME

Now that you know what you Do Want for your body, we'll focus on your home. This is a focus that's often overlooked, but our home environment has a huge effect on our well-being, and we all have the power to improve the energy of the space around us.

Let your home come into your awareness. Let any Don't Wants come into your mind, and thank them for directing you to their opposites.

Focus on the energy in your heart, and feel the presence of your Guardian Angel there. Connect to the power of the beautiful pattern of energy it holds for you concerning your home.

Supported by your Guardian Angel, spend a few moments deciding what you Do Want for your home.

Let yourself playfully think about why you want these things. Choose a word that describes the energy this change will bring to your home.

Now connect with the living energy that this word represents.

Do this from your heart, and keep doing it until you notice that your heart is feeling full and happy.

From this full and happy place, imagine a little scene in which you're living what you Do Want for your home.

When you're done, ground yourself into the love of the Earth. Notice how you feel emotionally, and notice how you feel in your body.

FOCUS ON WHAT YOU <u>WANT</u> FOR YOUR WORK

Now it's time to focus on your work. If you're not employed, then focus on what you consider to be your work in the world.

Let your work come into your awareness. Let any Don't Wants come into your mind, and thank them for directing you to their opposites.

Focus on the energy in your heart, and feel the presence of your Guardian Angel there. Connect to the power of the beautiful pattern of energy it holds for you concerning your work.

Supported by your Guardian Angel, spend a few moments deciding what you Do Want concerning your work. Relax while you think about why you want these things.

Focus on how you'd love to feel about your work or how fulfilled you feel when doing work you love. Keep doing this until you feel happy and empowered.

Choose a word that describes the energy the right work will bring into your life and into the world.

Now connect with the living energy that this word represents.

From this happy and empowered place, imagine a little scene in which you're living what you Do Want for your work. Don't worry about choosing the "perfect work"; feel free to play around with different ideas, as long as they all make you happy.

When you're done, ground yourself into the love of the Earth. Notice how you feel emotionally, and notice how you feel in your body.

FOCUS ON WHAT YOU <u>WANT</u> WITH MONEY

Now we're going to focus on money. It's time to create a brand-new relationship with money, knowing it as a Guardian energy directing abundance to us from the heart of the Earth.

Let the subject of money come into your awareness. Allow the Don't Wants about money to come into your mind (without getting too bogged down by them), and thank them for directing you to their opposites.

Focus on the energy in your heart, and feel the presence of your Guardian Angel there. Connect to the power of the beautiful pattern of energy it holds for you concerning your money.

Supported by your Guardian Angel, spend a few moments deciding what you Do Want in your relationship with money. Open your mind and heart as you let yourself playfully think about why you want these things.

Make it a game—focusing on how you love to feel certain ways or how it's fun to be able to do certain things. Do this from your heart, and keep doing it until you notice that your heart is feeling full and happy.

From this full and happy place, imagine a little scene in which you're living what you Do Want regarding money.

When you're done, ground yourself into the love of the Earth. Notice how you feel emotionally, and notice how you feel in your body.

FOCUS ON WHAT YOU <u>WANT</u> IN YOUR RELATIONSHIPS

Relationships are a huge part of our lives, and the positive changes we make in our relationships uplift everything in our lives.

Let a relationship come into your awareness. Let any Don't Wants about this relationship come into your mind, and thank them for directing you to their opposites.

Focus on the energy in your heart, and feel the presence of your Guardian Angel there. Connect to the power of the beautiful pattern of energy it holds for you concerning this relationship.

Supported by your Guardian Angel, spend a few moments deciding what you Do Want for this relationship. Relax while you think about why you want these things.

And now let yourself playfully think about why you want these things. Do this in a light way, focusing on how good it can feel to be together, or how satisfying it feels to accomplish things together. Do this from your heart, and keep doing it until you notice that your heart is feeling full and happy.

From this full and happy place, imagine a little scene in which you're living what you Do Want regarding this relationship.

When you're done, ground yourself into the love of the Earth. Notice how you feel emotionally, and notice how you feel in your body.

FOCUS ON WHAT YOU <u>WANT</u> FOR YOUR FUTURE

Now let's focus on your future.

Let a picture of your future come into your awareness. Allow the Don't Wants about your future to come into your mind, and thank them for directing you to their opposites.

Focus on the energy in your heart, and feel the presence of your Guardian Angel there. Connect to the power of the beautiful pattern of energy it holds for you concerning your future.

Supported by your Guardian Angel, spend a few moments deciding how you Do Want your future to unfold. Relax while you think about why you want these things.

And now let yourself playfully think about why you want these things. Do this in a light way, focusing on what you love to do and how you love to feel. Do this from your heart, and keep doing it until you notice that your heart is feeling full and happy.

From this full and happy place, imagine a little scene in which you're living what you Do Want in the future.

When you're done, ground yourself into the love of the Earth. Notice how you feel emotionally, and notice how you feel in your body.

FOCUS ON WHAT YOU <u>WANT</u> FOR THE WORLD

Finally, we'll focus on the world. This can involve our governments, people across the world, and the well-being of the planet itself.

Let the world come into your awareness. Allow the Don't Wants about the world to come into your mind, and thank them for directing you to their opposites.

Focus on the energy in your heart, and feel the presence of your Guardian Angel there. Feel the presence of Angels spread out across every part of the planet, and connect to the power of the beautiful pattern of energy they hold for the world.

Spend a few moments deciding what you Do Want for the world.

Let yourself playfully think about why you want these things. Do this in a light way, focusing on what you love about the world and the people in it. Do this from your heart, and keep doing it until you notice that your heart is feeling full and happy.

From this full and happy place, imagine a little scene in which you're living or observing what you Do Want for the world.

When you're done, ground yourself into the love of the Earth. Notice how you feel emotionally, and notice how you feel in your body.

Now that you've taken the time to get clear on what you Do Want, it will be easier to switch your focus when you catch yourself focusing on what you Don't Want.

Remember that the love in your heart is a powerful force for good in the world, and by attuning to it this way, you become a more powerful force for good.

CHAPTER 22

⚬⚭⚬

CLAIM YOUR BOUNDARIES

Healthy boundaries define your personal physical, emotional, and energetic space.

Read that again, more slowly, so that you can connect to the meaning in every part of the sentence. Healthy boundaries define your personal *physical, emotional,* and *energetic* space.

One easy-to-understand example of a healthy boundary (which is also an example of our natural individuality) is the skin on our bodies. Each one of us is held intact physically with a boundary of skin that makes it really easy to see where we start and where someone else stops. If only it were that easy emotionally and energetically!

We've all heard about boundaries, and most of us have read plenty of articles about how important it is to have good boundaries, but it can be really hard to put this advice into practice. So in this chapter and the next, we'll go into depth with the subject of boundaries. We'll talk about the underlying issues that make it hard for us to know and express our own boundaries (let alone enforce them). You'll get a deeper understanding of the whole issue of boundaries and how the issue relates to you. From there, you'll move on to discover exactly what your unique personal boundaries are, and we'll talk about how you can enforce your own boundaries in ways that will improve your life.

Your boundaries express the fact that you are a separate, unique individual, and this brings us to the first underlying issue. On one level, it feels good to be a separate, unique individual. But underneath, we sometimes feel uncomfortable feeling "separate." We're often taught that it's not emotionally safe to be separate, and we tend to energetically and emotionally mesh with the people we love.

Many of us are so good at merging with others that we become overly affected by other people's emotions and desires. We don't—all the way deep down—feel it's truly a good thing to be a separate, unique individual, because we're not sure that it's safe.

So let's start by simply bringing that thought to our awareness.

Deep down, do you feel that you can be a separate, unique, authentic individual and still have the wonderful, fulfilling types of relationships we all seek? Another way of saying that is, do you believe you can express your true boundaries and have others love you (the way you want to be loved) at the same time?

Play around with this idea, and see what thoughts and feelings come up.

YOUR EXPERIENCE WITH BOUNDARIES

Stop now and take a moment to think about the issue of boundaries in your own life.

How do you feel about the issue of boundaries, period?

What has been your experience with boundary-setting in your life so far? Where in your life do you have good, clear boundaries?

Where in your life are you comfortable expressing how you authentically feel about:

- *What's right for you?*
- *How you like to be treated?*
- *What you will and will not do?*

Where in your life are you not comfortable expressing how you authentically feel about:

- *What's right for you?*
- *How you like to be treated?*
- *What you will and will not do?*

As always, just asking yourself these questions will begin a process of change and greater empowerment. You don't have to have solutions—just asking the questions is enough right now.

BOUNDARY SIGNALS

The subject of boundaries can be confusing. We tend to think of boundaries as something we construct, but I like to think of them as natural borders that are already in place within us.

They delineate not only our personal space, but also the ways of being that are right for us.

Sometimes we don't consciously know what our personal boundaries are, because they are not something we've been taught to focus on (in fact, most of the time we're taught to *ignore* our own boundaries).

But our boundaries come with built-in signals that tell us when something's not right for us, and one of the most common signals is anger.

You can always tell where your boundaries are being violated by looking at the situations that make you angry.

Think back to the last time you were mad. Can you identify the boundary that was violated?

How did you deal with the boundary violation?

Now think back to a time when your feelings were hurt. Can you identify the boundary that was violated?

How did you deal with that boundary violation?

As you mull this over, open your awareness to a new way of looking at boundaries.

CREATING YOUR FOUNDATION

As you become more comfortable claiming and enforcing your boundaries, you'll be aligning more and more with your own divine blueprint. You're creating a conscious connection with your own soul purpose, and drawing from its powerful energy.

But don't think you have to start expressing or enforcing all your boundaries right away. Most of us have trouble communicating *all* our boundaries, and this book isn't about forcing yourself to do anything you're not ready to do.

Right now we're focusing on getting clear with ourselves about what our boundaries are, because that will create the foundation each one of us needs in order to be able to naturally communicate them. It's okay to take small, steady steps, becoming more and more aware of your true boundaries as you continue to tune in to your authentic self.

I'm not an advocate of forcing yourself to make radical change, because the changes you're not ready for *don't stick.* But small, incremental steps lead to lasting change, because they give you time to adjust along the way.

Take a deep breath, and go within for a moment. Feel your Guardian Unicorns at your sides, and see their radiance lighting up every part of you. In that light, see your own divine blueprint as a pattern spread throughout your body and energy system.

Take in another fresh, deep breath, and see the pattern glow more brightly within you.

Your personal boundaries—the ways of being that are right for you—help you express and stay true to that sacred pattern.

WHERE BOUNDARIES ARE HARDEST TO SET

Boundaries are hardest to set in the situations where we feel the least worthy.

As with so many things in our lives, the issue of boundaries is really about self-worth. Whatever fears we have about setting boundaries can usually be traced back to a feeling of not being worthy, and that's especially true in our close personal relationships.

We may even be afraid that we'll lose the other person if we're completely honest about our boundaries. (If we did feel completely worthy, that fear would not exist.)

In the next chapter we'll take a step-by-step, nuts-and-bolts approach to expressing our boundaries, but right now we're creating a strong foundation for ourselves, and the first step is to feel worthy of having our boundaries and to place value in our authentic feelings.

It takes a leap of faith for most of us to believe that we're meant to follow our authentic feelings, that our feelings matter, and that they can guide us truly. But there's a rightness to living from our authentic selves that makes everything work out for us in a way that nothing else can.

So to begin, just allow yourself to become aware of the places in your life where you're not feeling worthy of expressing your boundaries. As always, that awareness will begin a process of transformation and empowerment for you.

BOUNDARIES ON BOTH SIDES

Since most of us haven't been given permission to have boundaries or to believe in the rightness of our authentic feelings, it makes sense that it's hard to openly *express* our boundaries. But when we don't have openly expressed boundaries, we often resort to manipulation (sometimes without even realizing it!).

This issue isn't just about *us* not having healthy boundaries, it's about most other people also not having healthy boundaries. If we're in a situation where we feel we can't openly express ourselves, healthy boundaries aren't present on *either* side.

When that's the case, we tend to resort to manipulation of one kind or another in order to get our needs met. This just adds to the dysfunction, and keeps us from living and expressing our divine blueprint.

It also gets in the way of creating true, heart-to-heart relationships. On top of all of this, it's disempowering, because *anytime we can't deal with something in an open way, it disempowers us.*

If we don't allow ourselves to claim and enforce our own boundaries, we often end up building emotional walls around us in an effort to keep from getting hurt.

With this in mind it's easier to see why boundaries are such an important component to all our relationships, from the least important and casual to the most important and meaningful.

Authentic boundaries need to be in place on both sides of a relationship. Of course, each one of us can only be in charge of ourselves. But when you introduce health into any situation, it creates a resonance that causes a chain reaction, rippling out to everything.

Take a moment to think about the boundaries that exist, on both sides, of one of your casual relationships.

Now think about the boundaries that are expressed in your most important relationship. Set an intention to simply begin noticing the boundaries that exist in all your relationships.

A NEW PERSPECTIVE ON YOUR BOUNDARIES

I hope this chapter has brought you a greater grasp of the underlying issues that affect your ability to express and enforce your personal boundaries.

In the next chapter, we'll begin talking about actual boundary communication techniques. Let's prepare for that now.

Bring to mind the relationship in your life that most needs better boundaries.

What, specifically, would you like to change in this relationship?

What do you feel in your body as you think about this?

Call on the presence of your Guardian Dragon and ask for help setting and enforcing healthy boundaries within this relationship. Be open to this help coming in multiple ways: in new ideas, new thoughts, new understandings, new feelings, and even in changed circumstances.

Now that you have a better understanding of what's been keeping you from being able to express your boundaries, you can use that understanding to transform the issue, empowering yourself to use boundaries to make your life safer, happier, and more fulfilling.

A LONG WAY FROM MASTERY—BUT WORKING ON IT

Believe me, I'm a long way from mastery when it comes to boundaries—but I've learned that calling on my Guardians leads to much more positive outcomes.

One example is a boundary violation I experienced recently while writing this book. Even though my house is medium size with four bedrooms, it's considered a town house, which means I have a shared wall with my next-door neighbor, Bonnie.

Bonnie is kind of a grouch, but I give her a pass because she's an animal lover. The walls between our houses are very well insulated, and in all the years I've lived here I've never heard any music, TV, or sounds of talking coming from Bonnie's house.

Until two weeks ago, when Bonnie's grown grandson moved in with her. One day, soon after his arrival, I was working in my home office (a room with a shared wall) without a care in the world, when all of a sudden the sound of music came blaring through the wall.

I had no idea it was even possible for sounds to come through the wall that loudly, and the fact that my private space was being invaded made me so mad, so fast! I sat there stewing, trying to work but feeling distracted by the sounds coming through the wall.

Here's the interesting part: even though my boundary was clearly being violated, it seems that it wasn't enough of a violation to motivate me to take action in that moment.

The only action I could imagine was to march over to Bonnie's front door and tell her that the music was bothering me. I could imagine easily taking that action if I were in the process of making an audio recording (in which case, the desired outcome—a quiet space to record—would outweigh the discomfort of having an awkward conversation).

But apparently my anger at having my writing space invaded did *not* outweigh the cost of confronting Bonnie, so I simmered quietly as I worked.

Part of the problem was that I'm a natural diplomat. (It must also be said that I dislike confrontation as much as the next person.) I didn't want to knock on her door and accuse her of something (which was all I could think of doing). When people are accused, they naturally become defensive, so I always try to approach people in a way that allows the other party to save face. Without knowing something to say that felt right and good to me, I let my boundary be violated.

Then the loud music came through my wall again, and again a few days later. This time I came to my senses and asked my Guardian Dragon for help. I "gave the situation over," thinking of my Dragon Guardian every time I noticed the music.

Within a few minutes, a new idea popped into my head. I could ask Bonnie and/or her grandson if perhaps they had a speaker placed against our shared wall. I could mention the fact that everything was usually so quiet—which I appreciated because I need a quiet space in which to work—and now I was wondering what strange anomaly could possibly be causing the transfer of sound between our two residences!

I jumped up, walked downstairs, out my front door down to the sidewalk, and back up to Bonnie's front door. I rang the doorbell, but there was no answer. I could see that there were no lights on inside the house, and I began to wonder if Bonnie had gone away on a trip (which would explain a lot).

By the time I got back to my home office, the music had stopped, and as of this writing (a few weeks later), it has not resumed. There is no doubt in my mind that my Guardian Dragon gave me the idea that popped into my head, and I'm confident that if the musical violation (or any other boundary violation) occurs, I can partner with the Dragons to achieve a positive outcome.

I just have to remember to reach out to them.

CHAPTER 23

~ఌఌ~

ENFORCE YOUR BOUNDARIES

In the previous chapter we talked about the value of healthy boundaries and the underlying issues that make having healthy boundaries difficult. The steps in this chapter will show you how to begin a practice of expressing and enforcing healthy boundaries.

It seems to me that a lack of awareness of how to communicate boundaries *in a way that feels right and good to us* is one of the major blocks we have to enforcing our natural boundaries.

We don't just want to be rude or confrontational or get in a big power struggle—and we often don't know any other way. And so a lot of times we just push our boundaries down and try to ignore them.

It will help if you look at this as a skill you are developing, instead of something you should have already (magically!) mastered. Like everything else, setting and enforcing boundaries is a skill you can learn and improve on with practice.

The first step is to become aware of what your boundaries are (we began working on that in the last chapter). The next step is to recognize and acknowledge each boundary violation to yourself as it's happening.

Remember that our internal boundaries are not something that need to be created; *they are already naturally there.* When we're involved in situations that are right for us, we feel good—we feel *right*. This doesn't mean that we feel "right" while the other person is "wrong"; it means that we feel a sense of rightness within us, a feeling of being balanced and centered.

When we don't feel good and right, our feelings are a signal that whatever is happening is violating one of our natural boundaries.

We're not taught to honor our boundaries; we're taught to go along, be polite, and basically do what makes *everyone else* feel better.

So a vital key to this process is to *not doubt what you're feeling*. Honor your feelings—honor the awareness of your natural boundaries.

And when you do encounter a boundary violation—when someone says something that makes you feel disrespected or put down, when you receive a request for something that you really don't want to fulfill, when you're hearing comments around you that don't feel good, when you're being criticized in a way that feels bad, or when you're in a conversation and the topic makes you uncomfortable—acknowledge that you have a personal boundary, and whatever's going on is crossing that boundary.

For now, it's enough to just acknowledge it to yourself.

Think back to a recent time when one of your boundaries was crossed.

Be fully in your body, fully inside your own self, feeling your emotions and only your emotions, responsible only for your own feelings and actions. Then imagine yourself just acknowledging to yourself that one of your boundaries is being crossed.

Connect through your heart to the energy of your own soul purpose. Know that you're becoming more and more aware of what's right for you and what's not right for you by the way you feel. Get clear on exactly what it is that's not feeling right for you.

And ground down into the Earth, knowing that it's enough now to just be aware. Day by day, you'll gain more skill.

Acknowledge yourself for being brave enough to look at the truth of your own boundaries, and know that I'm sending you love!

ACTIVATE THE ENERGY OF WHAT'S RIGHT FOR YOU

Along with recognizing and acknowledging each boundary violation to yourself as it's happening, the second step involves determining what's right for you (what you would like *instead*) as the boundary violation is happening.

If it's a case of not being treated with respect, then recognize that—even if you don't feel able to fully express it in the moment. Being treated with disrespect is a hard one for most of us. We haven't been taught the words to address it.

We don't necessarily want to talk about how we feel or get involved in a debate that's off-topic.

We just want to stick up for ourselves in a way that feels healthy and empowered.

I think what we *really* want is for people to treat us with respect from the get-go! But when that's not the case, you can begin developing your boundary-enforcing skills by mentally acknowledging the boundary violation and then thinking of the way you would like to be treated instead.

For example, if you're in a situation where you're not being treated with respect and you don't feel comfortable saying anything (or you don't know what to say), acknowledge that it's happening, and think of how you *would* like to be treated. In that moment, activate the energy of what's right for you *inside of you*. Think of an example of when you *were* being treated with respect, and bring that memory forward into your being in the present.

It's important to do this even when dealing with trivial boundary violations. For example, one day I was at a gas station getting ready to pump my gas when I decided to also pay for a car wash. When I was done with the transaction at the gas pump, I saw that I'd been charged for a much more expensive car wash than I'd asked for.

I left my car and walked into the gas station to find two men: one behind the counter, and the other talking to him as if he were a friend.

I told the man behind the counter what had happened, and asked him what I needed to do to fix it. He waved his hand dismissively in my direction, said in a rude tone, "Just cancel it!" and turned his back to continue the conversation with his friend.

"Oh great," I thought, feeling disrespected. "He's *that* kind of guy."

By the time I got back to the gas pump, the car wash was filling up, so I decided to put the wash off for another time.

As I pumped my gas, I thought about the way I'd felt talking to the man inside the gas station. It wasn't the kind of boundary violation that I needed to address with *him* (no use!), but it was something I needed to address inside myself in order to get back to a state of inner balance.

I deliberately thought about the ways I like to be treated: with warmth and respect and friendliness. I thought about other times when I'd been treated really well. As I focused on these things, I felt my vibration returning to normal, and I felt good again.

By this time, my tank was full, and I left the gas station and continued running errands. And on my way home a few hours later, I noticed another gas station with a car wash.

I walked inside and asked the man behind the counter, "How do you pay for the car wash?" He was so polite and friendly—the perfect example of how I like to be treated.

You may be thinking this is an insanely trivial matter (or you may be thinking, "Kim—you need to figure out how car washes work!"), but the skill of recognizing your boundaries, claiming them, validating them, and getting in alignment with them inside your own mind will strengthen you and make it possible for you to shine so much more in the world.

That's all there is to it for step two. We're taking this in small steps so we can ground and integrate the practice of setting boundaries. This process is about finding a way that feels right to each one of us, a way of knowing and communicating that feels graceful and empowered. At its core, boundary setting is really just honest communication, and the first step—as with anything—is to get honest with ourselves.

SAYING NO

Now let's prepare to put our own guidance into action when it comes to saying no.

Some boundary violations come in the form of requests—those times when someone wants you to do something for them, and you immediately get that feeling in your gut that lets you know you don't want to do it.

Our new approach to boundaries involves getting clear on what (if anything) you *are* willing to do. This will involve leap-frogging over an old pattern you may have.

When we receive an unwelcome request, many of us experience two feelings at once: our immediate gut feeling—that we don't want to do whatever's being asked of us—and on top of that, a feeling that comes from our social conditioning (including the things we've been taught about what we should do).

We usually lay those "should" feelings on top of our gut feelings. We lay all the rules about what we "should" do on top of our authentic guidance. And so a lot of times we say yes when we want to shout no!

We fulfill the request that our authentic feelings are guiding us against, and that sets off a chain reaction. This is a chain reaction of things that don't work out, because we've made an *initial choice* that goes against our guidance.

Whenever we go against our authentic guidance, things don't work out the way we really want them to in the long run.

I can't stress enough how important it is to know that your authentic self is guiding you in the form of your gut feelings. I believe your guidance comes in the form of what you would love to do and what feels good in each moment. When I say "what feels good," I mean the choice you're *inspired* to do in that specific moment.

This goes directly against what a lot of us were taught. Many of us have been taught *not* to trust our feelings, *not* to trust what feels good, and to actually fear that if we do follow our feelings we'll end up running amok.

But here's what I believe: if we learn to follow our inner guidance in the form of our true feelings, we will create beautiful lives that express what we love and who we truly are.

If you begin to follow the authentic guidance coming from your Greater Self, the wisdom of that Greater Self will guide you (through what feels good) to the right choice in every situation.

That choice will actually benefit everyone, even if it doesn't seem like it in the moment.

Part of what makes it hard to enforce our boundaries is a belief that we have to be responsible for other people's feelings and well-being. We get stuck trying to make everything good for everyone around us (while pleasing everyone at the same time), and our own guidance gets lost in the shuffle.

We may also worry that we're being selfish at the expense of others.

It helps to know that our inner guidance is connected to a greater wisdom, a force that is working on behalf of *everyone*. When you make a decision that runs counter to your guidance (such as saying yes when you want to say no), then you actually block the flow of good that's waiting to come into the situation.

I believe that if it's not right for you, it's not truly right for the other people involved either, whether they know it or not.

If this resonates with you, give yourself permission to start honoring your own guidance more and more. Even when it involves saying no to someone, following your guidance brings a flow of powerful good into every situation.

SUPPORT YOURSELF

Support yourself through this process. Expressing and enforcing boundaries is a skill that most of us haven't been taught, and we need to be patient with ourselves as we learn it—and as we practice it.

We're going through a process of overcoming fears that have kept us from enforcing our boundaries. When you feel that your boundaries are being violated—even if you're not sure what to say, or even if you're in a situation where you're not feeling it's possible to say anything—support yourself in the boundary-setting process by matching your tone of voice and your facial expression to your boundary.

For instance, if you're in a situation where you don't feel there's anything you can say that would change the situation (or you don't know what to say), notice if you are smiling when you don't really feel like smiling, or if your tone of voice sounds cheerful even though you are unhappy. Begin matching your tone of voice and your facial expression to how you truly feel.

This isn't meant to be a ploy, but instead a step toward being true to yourself and coming into alignment with what's right for you.

When we don't express our boundaries, we betray ourselves, and that's what causes the true damage. This betrayal increases our feelings of insecurity and makes it harder to navigate through life.

When we ignore our own boundaries and pretend to feel differently than we do, we start to believe that we can't trust ourselves to keep ourselves safe or to create situations that feel right to us.

That's why matching the sound of your voice and the look on your face to how you *feel* when your boundaries are crossed is a good beginning step. It's especially useful when you're feeling disrespected, but you don't know what to do about it in the moment.

If you're not at the point where you have the right words to say or the right action to take, then begin the process of expressing your boundaries by matching your tone of voice and your facial expression to your boundary. Recognize what your boundary is, acknowledge it to yourself, and match your physical being with what you're really feeling authentically inside.

You'll be amazed at just how much that helps to jump-start this process and how much better, safer, and stronger you'll feel just by giving yourself permission to do it.

The biggest part of this process is allowing yourself to have the boundary—and not feeling that you need to justify it or have it approved by anyone else.

You are worthy of all your boundaries!

VERBALLY ENFORCING YOUR BOUNDARIES

The next step is to reach the point where you're comfortable verbally enforcing all your boundaries. Most of us are easily able to verbally enforce our boundaries in some areas of our lives and not at all comfortable expressing ourselves in others. Apply these suggestions to the places where you still have issues, and always follow your own guidance.

We'll start with this key: when you are verbally enforcing a boundary, do it clearly, calmly, and in as few words as possible. You don't want to get in a big debate or conversation, and you're not asking for permission. You're just gracefully, calmly, and firmly stating "what's what."

The clearer you are about your boundary, the easier this process will be. That's why all our preparatory work has been so important.

Knowing what your boundaries are is just the beginning. Making sure that your boundaries are respected is a vital step, so before we go further, let's take a moment to talk about the word *enforce*.

It's a hot word for a lot of people, because it seems overly masculine and too strong. Give yourself some time to think about that word and see where you stand on the idea of enforcement.

I'm going to keep using the word *enforce* because I think it's a good word to be comfortable with. Some synonyms for the word *enforce* are *administer*, *implement*, and *carry out*. Enforcing your boundaries doesn't have to be a battle, and you don't need to use *too much* force, but you *do* need to give yourself permission to express your truth.

One way to look at this is: if someone came and stood on your foot, you wouldn't shoot him with a gun, and you wouldn't punch him in the face—that would be using too much force.

You would start by simply telling him, and if he wasn't hearing you or didn't understand, you might actually reach out and gently push him off your foot. You would use exactly the amount of energy that you need to enforce that particular boundary.

That's what we want to aim for when we're verbally enforcing our boundaries. So again, be clear, be calm, and use as few words as possible, because *this is not a debate.* You are not explaining, and you're not asking for permission.

One thing that really helps when we do this is to speak from our diaphragm. When our voices are high, we're usually not coming from an empowered state. So, speak from your gut. Lower your voice a little if possible.

That will support you in this process. Get in an empowered, grounded place, remember not to ask for permission, and resist the urge to apologize.

When we go into a big explanation, what we're really doing is trying to get permission and make sure everyone still likes us. These are ways we've often been taught to navigate the world, but we've outgrown that now, and it doesn't serve us.

When we find ourselves apologizing or justifying a boundary, it means that *it's a weak boundary.* It's something we haven't really come to terms with ourselves, and we don't truly believe we have the right to have (and enforce) that boundary.

Play around with these ideas in your mind at first, and see where they lead you. As you do, observe yourself gently and with love.

CRYSTAL-CLEAR BOUNDARIES

When you get into an argument or debate about a boundary, it means you're allowing the other person to help you decide what your boundary is.

Just think about that for a moment.

Other people aren't connected to our own inner guidance and the wisdom of our authentic feelings, so it doesn't serve us to let anyone else get involved in setting our personal boundaries.

If possible, think in advance about how you want to clearly and succinctly state a new boundary. If the other person begins to enter into an argument with you to try to change your mind, resist the temptation to address whatever it is that they're bringing up. Simply restate your clear boundary.

This can be an uncomfortable process because it reinforces the negative programming that tells us we are not allowed to choose our own boundaries.

Sometimes when I express a boundary that's out of my comfort zone, it leaves me feeling uncomfortable afterward. I've even noticed that sometimes I'll leave the new boundary in place, but I'll allow (or even encourage) the person involved to encroach on some of my other boundaries, to kind of balance out the situation. Ack!

Observe yourself, and if you notice yourself doing the same thing, simply be aware, because that awareness is a powerful agent for positive change.

You deserve to have whatever boundaries feel right to you, and when you're crystal clear on the validity of your boundary, other people feel it.

For instance, when my kids were little, I never had a problem getting them to strap into their car seats or wear their seatbelts. (They fought me on a whole bunch of other issues, but never that one.) I believe it was because I was *100 percent convinced* that car seats and wearing seatbelts was a necessity.

One of my girlfriends wasn't as clear on that particular boundary as I was, and her kids sensed it. It was always a struggle getting them safely strapped in. (Believe me, I'm not bragging. Those same seatbelt-fighting kids followed their ultra-neat mother's rules about cleaning up toys much better than mine did!)

Take a moment and see if you can identify some similar instances in your own life.

When you are crystal clear on the *validity* of your boundary, other people can feel it, and they naturally tend to respect it.

SAMPLE BOUNDARY STATEMENTS

Boundaries are simply honest communication, and when we're not feeling safe to communicate honestly, that's a problem we need to address. You deserve to live according to the natural, authentic way of being that's right for you, and your boundaries are an important part of the better life you're creating.

We'll end our focus on boundaries with some sample boundary statements. As I go through them, you may be inspired to create your own. If so, write them down. (It's good to have some boundary statements stored in your memory bank so that you can easily access them when you need them!)

It's easy to state a boundary with somebody you don't know or don't like, but we're focusing on the conversations we have with people with whom we have ongoing relationships. We want those conversations to be graceful as well as empowered.

When you state a boundary, you're basically saying what you won't do and then (if you like) what you will do.

So begin to think in terms of first stating what you *won't* do (you don't need to state why), then stating what you *will* do. In terms of requests, you might say (fill in the blank) won't work for me, but I'd be happy to (fill in the blank).

The key part of this statement is the part where you say (fill in the blank) won't work for me or doesn't work for me. For instance, if you want me to take your kids for the weekend, I can say, "Watching the kids won't work for me, but I'll be happy to (fill in the blank)." (And that's only if there is something I *would* be happy to do at another time.)

If you're asked to do something that you actually aren't opposed to in general, but your guidance isn't telling you that you want to do it right now, you can say, "(Fill in the blank) doesn't work for me this time, but ask me again in the future!"

Notice that saying something "doesn't work" or "won't work" is not the same as giving an explanation. Most of the time, you really don't owe people an explanation.

The clearer you are about your feelings, and the more you support yourself in following your guidance on what feels right for you, the easier it is to simply state what works and what doesn't work (without going into long explanations).

A lot of times, our long explanation is a kind of request for others' agreement and approval, and many times we offer it in hopes that we won't hurt their feelings or that they won't be mad at us.

Another thing you can say is, "(Fill in the blank) won't work for me, but I wish you all the best with your project" (or whatever it is that they're doing). This works well when you are saying no, and there isn't something else you are willing to do.

In that case, going back to our earlier example, try: "Watching the kids won't work for me, but I'll hold a good thought that someone else is available!"

When you're really not sure about a request, or someone takes you by surprise and you can't get it all figured out in the moment, you can enforce your boundaries by saying, "I'm not sure; I'll have to think about it."

When you're feeling put down, you can say, with as little emotion as possible, "This conversation needs to be respectful." Don't be surprised if you find yourself having to repeat this one. Again, the clearer *you* are, the easier it will be.

The other day I was standing outside a store waiting for it to open, and a disheveled man walked up. Even though he didn't look particularly threatening, I instinctively connected with the presence of my Guardian Dragon.

The man smiled and said, "Hello." I said, "Hello," back, and then he looked at me and said a really offensive (and threatening) comment. Wow!

I'm usually guided to ignore these types of events, but this time I surprised myself by looking him in the eye and saying, "Go away!" in a deep voice. (It must have been the Dragon's influence!) He walked away so fast! He kept looking back over his shoulder, like he didn't really want to walk away, but he couldn't help himself.

It feels so good to be able to speak up and express your boundaries.

Play around with our sample boundary statements, create new ones that will work for you in your life, and begin to put them into practice. Becoming aware of boundaries, setting boundaries, and enforcing your boundaries is a skill, and like any skill, you'll get better at it with practice.

This is definitely a journey! Know that you deserve to have all your boundaries respected and that I'm sending you love. Remember, we're in this together!

CHAPTER 24

<small>ᦒᦒ</small>

BECOME A CARETAKER OF CONSCIOUSNESS

We'll begin this chapter with a premise: *everything* has its own energy field and its own consciousness.

Objects can carry outside energies that have been impressed upon them (just as rooms hold the positive or negative energies that have been expressed inside them), but I believe they *also* have their own inherent consciousness.

I've always intuitively felt this to be true, and I was so excited to find more about this subject in my friend David Spangler's awesome book, *Subtle Worlds: An Explorer's Field Notes.*

Most people consider inanimate objects to be nonliving things, but I'm going to ask you to open your heart to the possibility that *everything* is alive with its own "being-ness." When you take time to connect and commune with any object, you participate in the co-creative tapestry of life in a magical way.

You probably already have the intuitive sense that something doesn't have to be biological in order to be alive. There are many different types and levels of consciousness. In Chapter 6 of *Subtle Worlds*, David Spangler says:

"When I look around me at the things in my world and say, 'Everything is Alive,' what I'm really saying is that everything is consciousness in a process of evolution." He goes on to say, "We are each caretakers for the consciousness evolving around us, particularly those of a lesser complexity and capacity than our own."

You'll be experiencing this for yourself in the following pages, but stop and take a moment now to check in with your own feelings about this idea, noticing any wisdom or insights that come to you.

CREATE A HEART CONNECTION

When you love something, it begins to love you back.

You can begin to experience this by randomly choosing an object that's in front of you right now. Make sure this is a human-made object, not a crystal or stone.

I'm sitting at my desk right now, and I see pens, pencils, my computer mouse, my mouse pad, and my keyboard before me.

I'll choose a pen to use as our example today. This particular pen is a navy-blue Cross pen that my good friend Glennie gave me for Christmas.

I start by grounding myself into the love of the Earth, picking up the pen, and focusing all my attention on it. I open my mind to see the pen as a holder of its own consciousness. In doing this, I feel like I'm really seeing it for the first time, and I open my heart and shine love to this pen. I imagine that my love is enveloping and filling the pen.

Now I expand my awareness and tune in to the energy of the pen. The first thing I notice is the energy of Glennie's love wrapped around the pen. When I allow myself to go deeper, I intuitively feel the pen's own presence. It's a very simple presence, not like a human presence at all, but I can still feel it. I continue to send the pen my love, and I feel a heart connection being formed. Try this for yourself now.

Choose an object, ground yourself into the love of the Earth, and really see the object as you focus all your attention on it. Open your heart and shine love to this object. Now open your awareness and tune in to the energy of the object. Go past the outside energies that may be surrounding it, and intuitively tune in to its own inherent presence.

Create a heart connection with this object, and open yourself to any positive energies you feel coming back to you. You may feel these right away, or it may take time, but I'm willing to bet that as you look at this object right now, you feel a connection that wasn't there yesterday.

Love is the Miracle-Gro of the Universe, and your love helps the objects around you to evolve in their consciousness. As they do, you'll feel their love coming back to you.

THE REALITY BEYOND OUR FIVE SENSES

One day last year I was sitting across from Glennie in a restaurant talking about the consciousness of objects, and my eyes happened to fall on the knife that was lying next to my plate.

I picked it up and told Glennie that I believed this knife possessed its own consciousness. I opened my heart, connected to the knife with love—and the energy in our restaurant booth *changed*. There was a quality to the space that hadn't been there before—the change that always results when we open our eyes to the reality beyond our five senses.

I "made friends" with the knife, and suddenly all three of us—Glennie, the knife, and I—were uplifted. All of this occurred with an object I'll probably never see again; imagine what can unfold with objects that you interact with day after day!

Let's stay with the theme of silverware and begin a practice of making friends with the utensils we use. Go through it now with me in your imagination.

Ground yourself into the love of the Earth, and then imagine you're sitting at the dinner table. Pick up your fork, and focus all your attention on it. Open your heart and shine love to this fork.

Now open your awareness and tune in to the energy of the fork. Go past the outside energies that may be surrounding it, and tune in to its own inherent presence. Create a heart connection with this fork, and open yourself to any positive energies you feel coming back to you.

When you eat your next meal, go through this process in real life with your fork, knife, and spoon, and notice how the energy around the table changes!

YOUR FAVORITE CHAIR

Now let's devote some time to becoming aware of the energy of one of our favorite objects. (In his book, David Spangler uses the example of a sofa, but I have a comfy chair I love to sit in when I watch TV, so we'll use a chair for our exercise.)

Choose the chair you most like to sit in, and approach it as a living being today.

Ground yourself into the Earth's embrace, and feel yourself in your energetic house of self-love. Say, "I love myself," and take a moment to feel the energy of your own love.

Now stand in front of your favorite chair, and open yourself to its inherent presence. If you like, you can use your hands to sense its energy. What does it feel like to you?

Open your heart and shine love to this chair. Silently (or out loud) communicate with this chair, telling it what you love about it and how much you appreciate its presence. Create a conscious heart connection with the chair.

Finally, sit in the chair, and notice how it feels now that you have begun a loving relationship with it. Set the intention to consciously connect for a moment every time you sit in this chair.

CONNECT TO THE ACTUAL CONSCIOUSNESS

I was in my local grocery store the other day, and I noticed that they've installed bright-yellow Amazon Lockers near the checkout aisles. Amazon Lockers are alternative package pickup stations for amazon.com deliveries, and this set of lockers had "Hi, my name is Wendy" printed on it in big letters.

This got me thinking about the difference between what we've been doing in this chapter and anthropomorphizing. Anthropomorphizing is the act of attributing human qualities to an object or animal or other nonhuman thing.

Many of us like to relate to our things this way, naming our cars, for example. In one sense this is good, because it gives us a way to connect to the things around us with love. But the drawback is that we relate to these objects only in our own imaginations, rather than connecting to the *actual* innate consciousness of each thing.

For example, if I walked up to the bank of lockers and said, "Hello, Wendy!" with love, Wendy and I would have one kind of experience together. But if I looked past the name that humans had given this object-being, and had as my intention to connect with the essential consciousness of this object, the bank of lockers and I would have a much deeper, richer experience.

Of course, as I said before, this kind of consciousness is very simple and different from our own, but by relating to it in its essential form, I allow space for our relationship to evolve beyond the borders of my own thoughts and fancies.

Take a moment now to consider this for yourself, and take note of the quality of your interactions with the objects around you today.

GOING DEEPER

Now that you've had a chance to connect with some objects, let's go even deeper into the process. We'll use a coffee mug as our example. I love to collect coffee mugs (even though I drink tea instead of coffee). Whenever I go someplace new, this is my souvenir of choice.

Every morning I go to my mug cupboard and spend a moment choosing which mug feels right for that particular day. Some mugs have logos (like from restaurants or Disneyland), and some have pictures (like the mug I got at the top of the John Hancock building in Chicago).

Some are mugs that I've received as gifts (like a Unicorn mug from my son, Jimmy), and some represent whole cities (like my favorite Starbucks San Francisco mug).

Let's use that mug as an example. If I open myself to the energy of the mug, I might first come into contact with outside energies that the mug is carrying. For instance, if I received it as a gift, I might feel the love of the person who gave it to me.

The mug in my example might hold some of the energy of the city it represents, since the San Francisco skyline is represented on the mug's surface, and the name of the city is printed on the inside of the cup.

In a similar way, it might carry within it the energy of the company it represents: Starbucks. Going deeper, I might find the energy of "cup" itself, the same energy and intention that is in all cups, everywhere.

And beneath all of that is the consciousness of this individual cup. That energy is what I can choose to connect to and foster and love.

You might not consciously feel all the aforementioned energies when you connect with an item. But it's good to know that they may be there as you start connecting with some of your favorite items.

JUST THE BEGINNING

We've come to the end of this chapter, but I hope it's just the beginning of a new way of life: loving (and being loved by) everything around us.

Think of the objects you've connected with as you journeyed through this chapter. Create a new habit of connecting to them with love every time you see them. In addition to that, create a daily practice of connecting with love to the consciousness of one new thing every morning.

Take a moment now, open your heart to the objects around you, and jot down the items that pop into your head. Use this list to get started with your daily connection practice.

We began this chapter with the premise that everything has its own energy field and its own consciousness. As you recognize the consciousness in the things around you and continue to connect with love to each thing, you will truly become a caretaker of consciousness.

And in time, you will begin to feel that love and care coming back to you, surrounding you in an interconnected web of love and support.

CHAPTER 25

SUPPORT YOURSELF WITH LOVE

In this chapter we'll deepen our practice of sending ourselves Love, supporting ourselves with Love, and surrounding ourselves with Love. I've capitalized the word *Love* here to help remind us that it is not just a flowery sentiment or a nice emotion.

Love is the energy that creates, maintains, and runs the Universe, and by being willing to direct this flow of love to ourselves, we strengthen ourselves and take our places as more vibrant, vital parts of All That Is.

Remember, loving yourself brings you into alignment with the Guardian Beings who are waiting to help you fulfill your soul purpose. Coming from a strong foundation of loving yourself will support and empower you in being a powerful force for good in the world.

We'd probably all prefer to receive love from someone else than to receive it from ourselves. But we have to ask ourselves: If we don't feel worthy or willing to give and receive love from ourselves, how much are we truly open to receiving love from others?

Take in a nice, deep breath. Allow yourself to relax as you exhale, and use the power of your intention to create a safe, sacred space around you.

Now use this centering ritual: first, recognize your own value and power by centering yourself within your house of self-love and saying, "I love myself." Open to the presence of your Greater Self, and feel it fill you and spread out to fill your house of self-love.

Tune in to your own energy field, and call all your energy back into your body.

Drop energetic roots down into the Earth, and feel love and support flowing up to envelop you.

Focus on the energy of your own heart, and feel your own beautiful "energy signature."

Now connect to the energy of love. Feel it in your heart, and keep tuning in to its energy until its presence becomes stronger and stronger.

As we did in Chapter 6, imagine you're gazing at a child, pet, sweet baby animal, or anything that brings forth pure, flowing love. Imagine that you can see the energy of your love surrounding them in a circle. Now widen that circle until you are within the energy of your own love.

If this is hard, just relax, and gently open yourself to be in the space of this love, without thinking.

Now focus on the feeling of love within your heart, and feel it connecting to all the different parts of your body. Feel every part of you opening to happily receive this love.

Ground yourself into the loving Earth, and take a few moments to anchor in this feeling of self-love. Choose an activity that you can use today to remind you to take a few moments and repeat this experience. You could do it every time you wash your hands or use the restroom or whenever you sit down to eat, for example.

It's time to get more comfortable and adept at sending yourself loving energy. Celebrate the beginning of much more love in your life, knowing you have the power to bring it forth!

SEND YOURSELF LOVE

It may seem like a strange idea to "send" yourself love, but it can actually be a very powerful experience.

Before you go to sleep each night, think back over your day and watch the day's events like a movie in your mind. Send love to yourself in every situation you experienced, as if you were your own Guardian Angel.

Let's do this now, looking back at the events of yesterday. Again, we'll use our centering ritual as a foundation:

Recognize your own value and power by centering yourself within your house of self-love and saying, "I love myself." Open to the presence of your Greater Self, and feel it fill you and spread out to fill your house of self-love.

Tune in to your own energy field, and call all your energy back into your body.

Drop energetic roots down into the Earth, and feel love and support flowing up to envelop you. Focus on the energy of your own heart, and feel your own beautiful "energy signature."

Connect to the energy of love. Feel it in your heart, and keep tuning in to its energy until its presence becomes stronger and stronger.

Now look back to yesterday morning as if you are watching a movie starring you, and as you do, flow love to yourself. In your mind's eye, see yourself moving through your morning, and surround your yesterday self with the energy of love.

Now do the same thing with the afternoon. And now the evening.

Finally, see yourself tucked in bed last night, and send love straight from your heart in the present to surround your sleeping self with love and care.

This practice will have a cumulative effect, strengthening you from the inside out as it increases your sense of safety, happiness, and well-being.

SEND YOURSELF LOVE TODAY

Are you beginning to feel more comfortable with flowing love to yourself? I hope with all my heart that you are! We're going to add to your sense of comfort by filling one whole day with self-love. Complete this exercise upon first waking.

Start by connecting to the energy of love. Feel it in your heart, and keep tuning in to its energy until its presence becomes stronger and stronger.

Now think of something you're planning to do this morning. Picture yourself engaging in this activity as if you were watching a movie, and send love to yourself as you watch. See yourself relaxing as you receive this love. Notice the changes you feel in your physical body now, and notice any changes you observe in your future self as a result of this love.

Next, think of something you're planning to do this afternoon. Picture yourself engaging in this activity as if you were watching a movie, and send love to yourself as you watch.

Then think of something you're planning to do this evening. Picture yourself engaging in this activity as if you were watching a movie, and send love to yourself as you watch.

Finally, see yourself tucked in bed tonight, and send love straight from your heart in the present to surround your future sleeping self with love and care.

What do you feel in your body after sending this love? What do you notice about how your heart feels?

As you go through your day, continue to send love to your future self, and keep noticing any changes in the way you feel.

SEND LOVE TO YOUR CHILDHOOD SELF

Next, we'll send love back to a place where it's truly needed: your childhood.

Center yourself within your house of self-love and say, "I love myself." Open to the presence of your Greater Self, and feel it fill you and spread out to fill your house of self-love.

Tune in to your own energy field, and call all your energy back into your body.

Drop energetic roots down into the Earth, and feel love and support flowing up to envelop you. Focus on the energy of your own heart, and feel your own beautiful "energy signature."

Connect to the energy of love. Feel it in your heart, and keep tuning in to its energy until its presence becomes stronger and stronger.

Now let a scene from your childhood enter your mind. Picture yourself as a child within this scene, as if you were watching a movie, and send love to your child-self. Surround your child-self with the energy of love until it fills the entire scene.

Let another scene from your childhood enter your mind. Picture yourself as a child within this scene, as if you were watching a movie, and send love to your child-self. Surround your child-self with the energy of love until it fills the entire scene.

Once again, let another scene from your childhood enter your mind. Picture yourself as a child within this scene, as if you were watching a movie, and send love to your child-self. Surround your child-self with the energy of love, until it fills the entire scene.

Feel your child-self within your heart in the present, and send her love and appreciation for who she is.

This can be intense, so be gentle with yourself. Remember that I'm sending you love and seeing you surrounded with the energy of love in the present as well as the past!

SEND LOVE TO YOURSELF IN THE PAST

We'll continue on our journey of self-love by sending love back to ourselves during major events we've experienced. Don't let your mind get overinvolved in this process; your inner wisdom will bring to your awareness the memories that most need the energy of love.

Connect to the energy of love. Feel it in your heart, and keep tuning in to its energy until its presence becomes stronger and stronger.

Now let a scene from a significant event from your past enter your mind. Look back on this event as if you are watching a movie starring you, and as you do, flow love to yourself.

See yourself surrounded by Angels, Unicorns, Dragons, and loving Trees. Feel support flowing from the Earth, and continue to surround your past self with love.

Let another scene from a major event from your past enter your mind. Look back on this event as if you are watching a movie starring you, and as you do, flow love to yourself.

See yourself surrounded by Angels, Unicorns, Dragons, and loving Trees. Feel support flowing from the Earth, and continue to surround your past self with love.

Now let one more scene from your past enter your mind. Look back on this event as if you are watching a movie starring you, and as you do, flow love to yourself.

See yourself surrounded by Angels, Unicorns, Dragons, and loving Trees. Feel support flowing from the Earth, and continue to surround your past self with love.

The love you are sending to yourself is transforming you—and the past—in a powerful, lasting way. Hold the beautiful energy of this transformation within your being.

SEND LOVE TO YOUR "FAILURES"

Most of us carry around the old energies of what we consider to be failures from our past, and now we're going to send love to ourselves in these past situations.

As before, avoid letting your mind get overinvolved in this process. Your own inner wisdom will bring to your awareness the experiences of failure or loss that need to be transformed by love (and you may be surprised at what comes into your awareness).

This may or may not be intense, so be sure to follow your own guidance and set the intention to only bring to mind the situations you are ready to revisit.

Connect to the presence of Angels in the four corners of the room or space you are in. Feel the energy of their support and love.

Tune in to your own energy field, and call all your energy back into your body. Drop energetic roots down into the Earth, and feel love and support flowing up to envelop you.

Connect to the energy of love. Feel it in your heart, and keep tuning in to its energy until its presence becomes stronger and stronger.

Now, if it feels right, let a scene of a failure from your past enter your mind. Look back on this event as if you are watching a movie starring you, and as you do, flow love to yourself.

Notice any feelings that come up, but don't allow yourself to start thinking about this event in detail. Call on the Angels around you for support, and flow love to yourself without judgment.

Now, if it feels right, let another scene of a failure from your past enter your mind. Look back on this event as if you are watching a movie starring you, and again, flow love to yourself.

One more time, let a scene of a failure from your past enter your mind. Look back on this event as if you are watching a movie starring you, and as you do, flow love to yourself.

Now surround yourself with vibrant pink energy. Breathe it in, and feel a never-ending supply of this pink energy around you.

Continue to breathe in this beautiful pink energy as you go through the day. Drink plenty of water, and set an intention to release old energies that aren't in alignment with your divine blueprint. If some of the scenes from your past come into your mind, stop and take a few moments to send yourself love.

SEND LOVE INTO YOUR FUTURE

Finally, we'll send love to our future selves. This will take a different form for each of us, so try to keep your mind open to receive the "scenes" your inner wisdom brings to you.

Connect to the energy of love. Feel it in your heart, and keep tuning in to its energy until its presence becomes stronger and stronger.

Now imagine a possible scene of yourself in the future. Be relaxed and playful as you allow a possible version of "future you" to come into your mind. Now flow love and appreciation to your future self.

Imagine a different possible scene of yourself in the future. Look at this scene as if you're watching a movie starring you, and as you do, flow love and appreciation to your future self.

Now imagine one more possible scene of yourself in the future. Look at this scene as if you are watching a movie starring you, and as you do, flow love and appreciation to your future self.

Ground yourself into the love of the Earth now, and feel yourself in a stream of gorgeous pink-gold energy that flows through your past self, your present self, and your future self.

Allow this pink-gold energy to expand until it fills your world, and continue supporting yourself with love on an ongoing basis.

CHAPTER 26

EXPECT THE BEST WITH THE DRAGONS AT YOUR SIDE

There's one simple thing you can do right now that will begin to change everything in your life for the better: take control of your expectations.

Begin to align yourself with positive outcomes in your life by *expecting* to succeed in creating more of what you love. Start *deliberately* expecting the best.

If you're like most people, you probably think you already expect the best. But if you begin a daily, ongoing practice of reminding yourself to expect the best—success in your relationships, your work, your finances, your interactions with others—I think you'll be surprised at how often you catch yourself in the habit of expecting less than the best.

In fact, any time you experience a negative emotion, it's a sign that you're *not* expecting the best.

Life is meant to get better and better as you express more of who you are and what you love. But your life can only be as good as you allow it to be. If you believe that life is a mixture of highs and lows, good sprinkled with bad (or bad sprinkled with good), that is what life will be for you.

But it could be so much more.

IDENTIFY YOUR NEGATIVE EXPECTATIONS

Whenever you catch yourself feeling any form of anxiety, stop and ask yourself, "What is it that I am *expecting* in this situation?"

Close your eyes and think: Is there anything you feel stress or anxiety about right now? Get clear on exactly what's causing you stress.

Now take a deep breath, connect to the support of your Guardian Dragon, and uncover the expectation that's connected to your thoughts about this situation.

For example, if you're stressed about a project at work, your unconscious expectation may be that you won't finish in time or that the project won't be a success. If you're anxious about a relationship, your deep-down expectation might be that a loved one will reject you (or reject something about you).

Feel the presence of your Guardian Dragon now as you bring your true expectations into the light of your awareness.

The act of becoming aware of your true expectations is the first step to changing them.

BELIEFS AND EXPECTATIONS

Each one of us has a different set of beliefs, and each one of us is inhabiting a reality that is based on those beliefs.

Begin now to identify the sets of beliefs that form your expectations. Then you can decide if these expectations match who you *really* are—and who you want to become.

Your expectations are tied to your beliefs and your thought patterns, so sort through them and see which ones are right for you versus which ones you've inherited from your parents and your culture (or even an unconscious sense of not being good enough).

We tend to think of a belief as something that is set in stone, something we believe simply because it is "true." However, if you think back over your life, you'll probably see that your beliefs have changed over time.

Think about some of the things you used to believe, and see how, as you gained experience and your life expanded, you came to believe different things.

You are always in a state of evolution, growing in your own wisdom, knowledge, and understanding. Your beliefs evolve based on that.

If you find yourself holding on to a lot of negative or limiting beliefs, it simply means that your beliefs haven't yet evolved to match who you truly are.

You have the chance, right now, to release any beliefs that don't match who you are, and to identify and access new beliefs that do match who you are and who you are becoming.

When you find yourself holding a negative expectation, ask your Guardian Dragon to help you activate new beliefs within yourself that will help you live your best life. Do this in the form of a regular practice.

Connect with your Guardian Dragon at the same time every day (for example, every night at bedtime), and ask for help creating a new belief in a specific area of your life.

I think you'll be amazed at the changes you begin to see in yourself as your Guardian Dragon supports you in adopting new beliefs, new ideas, and new expectations.

These new beliefs and expectations will support you in every area of your life, connecting you to your Greater Self and the soul purpose that flows forth from that connection.

DRAGON EXPECTATION JOURNEY

The first time I took the following journey for myself, I expected to connect with my familiar Guardian Dragon. But the Dragon that appeared in my inner journey was an ancient sleeping Dragon who opened one eye and spoke to me very succinctly (almost grouchily, as if I should not need to ask!) about his expectation for me.

I treasured the experience and hold the wisdom I received from the Dragon in my heart to this day.

We all need support in upgrading our expectations, and having a direct experience of a Dragon Guardian's expectation for you is truly life changing.

Align yourself with your highest good, and ask to connect with a Guardian Dragon. Feel yourself grounded into the Earth's embrace, and go even deeper within.

Go deeper and deeper, until you come to a place where you see the familiar beautiful building, sparkling with magical energy. Notice your name engraved in large letters over the wide front doors.

Feel yourself entering this building now and standing in a huge, beautiful room filled with golden light. To your left you see a large bronze door, and you open it and step into a natural stone passageway.

You see small flames set into the walls to light your way, as well as thousands of tiny crystals that reflect the flickering light. You somehow know that you are deep within the Earth, and you follow the passageway until it opens onto a magnificent cave, with curving walls set with large crystals and gems.

You look up and see only blackness, but you get a sense that there is no ceiling, just open space that stretches all the way to the Earth's surface. There is a cozy fire burning, and in the center of the cave is a Guardian Dragon.

Look into its eyes with reverence, and feel your heart warm with thanks for the sense of welcome you feel. Continue to stand and look into this Dragon's eyes, connecting with its energy.

When it feels right, speak to this Guardian Dragon from your heart about a situation that is causing you anxiety. Now look into your heart and tell the Dragon what you would love to experience as an outcome of this situation.

Paint pictures with your words, making this outcome as beautiful as possible. You may even notice that in the situation you are imagining, this Guardian Dragon is present and part of your beautiful outcome.

When you are done, ask the Dragon if it will share with you its expectation for you. Open your heart and mind to receive this wisdom, in whatever form it takes.

Commune with this beautiful being for as long as you like. When you are ready, thank this Guardian Dragon, and if it feels right, ask it to stay connected with you in an energy of love and respect.

Most importantly, give it your blessing before you part.

Feel yourself fully in your body, move your arms and legs, and ground yourself once more into the love of the Earth as you return to your daily life, carrying a new, magical expectation in your body, mind, and spirit.

SPEND TIME REGULARLY VISUALIZING YOUR IMPROVED EXPECTATIONS

Now that you've experienced the power of a Guardian Dragon's expectations, it's time to step up and do some inner work to change your own energy patterns.

This takes the form of consistently imagining yourself experiencing improved outcomes. The purpose of this imagining is to match your thoughts and energy to the energy of your desired outcomes. (Our "Focus on What You *Want*" chapter has given you a head start with this!)

Think of an expectation you'd like to upgrade. In your mind and heart, imagine the outcome you'd like to expect. Imagine yourself physically experiencing that outcome, feeling the feelings that being in that experience would give you. Do this several times until your desired expectation feels more natural and more possible.

For instance, if you'd like to upgrade your expectation concerning your ability to save money, take a moment and imagine yourself in front of your computer screen, looking at your savings account statement as you'd like it to be.

Feel the presence of a Guardian Dragon in this scene, and ask it for its guidance to support you in all your creations.

Feel yourself in your body, sitting in your chair, looking at the screen. Get a clear sense of what it would feel like, and get grounded in that positive feeling.

Get that good feeling in your body as you see your financial statements. Feel your hand on the computer mouse, and hear yourself saying, "It feels so good to have (fill in your own amount) in savings!"

Connect to a feeling that there is "more to come," more good experiences like this one, positive experiences that will build on one another and create their own momentum.

You can match the energy of the things you desire by creating an experience in your imagination that matches the experience you want to create in real life. Feel how good it will feel, imagine yourself in the experience of having it, and match your energy to the situation you desire.

In that way, you'll begin to expect it. This new expectation will begin to change everything you think and do. It will change your personal energy, and you'll begin to see things that match the energy of your expectation show up in your life.

Begin in the morning and continue throughout the day to select the expectations you choose to hold, and match yourself to them.

CONNECT WITH THE SUPPORT OF THE DRAGONS

Everything always works out for me.
I am encircled by the wisdom
and love of the Dragons,
and my life is a shining light.

Make this your new expanded mantra. Say it not only when you feel anxious; get into the habit of saying it to yourself all day long.

This powerful thought will attract more thoughts like it, and begin to attract things and experiences that match it, and you will feel more and more connected to the Dragons as time goes on.

Your life is meant to evolve and expand in a positive way. When you don't achieve a desired outcome, imagine that a better result must be coming into place, because, "Everything always works out for me. I am encircled by the wisdom and love of the Dragons, and my life is a shining light."

When something happens that you don't like and you allow yourself to focus on it, you begin to match the energy of the unwanted thing and attract more things like it.

Instead, look at an undesired situation and change your focus to what you do want by saying, "Everything always works out for me. . . ."

By doing this, you put yourself back onto your own true path, traveling toward what you love. The things that are right for you can then more easily come into your experience.

Let the Dragons help you live the life that's right for you by *expecting* to succeed in creating more of what you love!

CHAPTER 27

~ॐ~

DREAM BIGGER

It's time to partner with the energy of expansion and bring that expansion to your visions and dreams—your heart's desires.

I believe your true heart's desires come from deep within you. They are blueprints of who you're *meant* to become. When you allow yourself to dream bigger, you open yourself up to embody more and more life force, and more and more of your Greater Self.

This is an important topic, because bigger dreams stretch us. They stretch us into becoming the bigger versions of ourselves that we are truly meant to be.

In a way, our dreams actually *define* us and act as guideposts on our path.

When we become disconnected from our dreams, we're cut off from the vision that comes from deep within us, the inner vision that illuminates our divine blueprint.

Center yourself in your heart and think of a time you felt fully alive, fully engaged, and filled with life. *That* was a time when you were showing up all the way.

That's what our dreams and visions do: they show us how to bring all our energy, love, and life force into the world, blessing it with the power of our authentic spirit.

As we go through this chapter, I'll support you in reconnecting with your power to dream, and guide you in connecting to the visions and heart's desires that are already inside you. You'll begin to come more and more into alignment with the beauty and magic within you as you connect to the power of your own dreams.

DREAMING FROM YOUR HEART

As we go through this chapter, you may ask yourself, "Isn't it wrong to dream bigger?" This is a valid question, so let's look at dreaming bigger versus being trapped in a state of always wanting more.

A feeling of constantly wanting more comes from the place of lack that exists when we're not expressing our true self. When we're cut off from the power source within us—when we're disconnected from our own truth and living from other people's rules—we have an emptiness inside that causes us to seek more and more.

By contrast, dreaming bigger comes from a place of getting in touch with the love in our hearts and expanding that love out into the world, where it can take physical form. It's about being in a natural state of personal evolution and expansion.

You can tell which state you're in by how you feel. Always needing more feels like hunger, as if you don't have something you need.

Dreaming from your heart feels like you *already* have something within you, and now you're being inspired to expand on that something and experience it in a fuller way.

We can be centered in the present and fully engaged with what we have in our lives now and *still* be inspired to create more.

Your dreams are instructions. Allow yourself to be guided by them, and ground yourself in the knowledge of all you are meant to do and be and have.

Get in touch with your heart, and think of all the things you're grateful for. Ground yourself in the good feeling of having.

Take a deep breath, feel the presence of all your Guardians supporting you, and ground yourself in the energy of love as you exhale.

That love connects you not only to the dreams and the visions you're meant to fulfill, but also to the love that powers the Universe.

You become a vehicle of that love as you allow yourself to dream bigger.

YOUR BIG DREAM

We know now how important it is to "give yourself permission," so today we'll focus on giving yourself permission to dream bigger.

Up until now, you might have been lacking your own permission to dream bigger because you may have felt it's wrong to ask for more than you have. (Now you know better!)

Or you may be comfortable with the idea of dreaming bigger, but disappointed because your dreams haven't yet taken form around you. Either way, take this moment to set an intention to give yourself new permission to dream.

What this really means is looking at your dreams in a new way.

Think of something outrageously wonderful that you would truly love to do or be or have, something that's very close to your heart. (More than one thing may come to mind, but just focus on one thing for now.)

Whatever that thing is, I believe that it's not something frivolous, and it's not something you shouldn't be asking for. Your dreams may involve people and places and things, but your dreams aren't really about anything outside you.

Your visions and dreams are really about creating a bigger, *truer* version of yourself. For instance, if someone has a dream to be wealthy, her dream is not really for the wealth itself, but for the possibilities and choices she'll experience as a wealthy person. Her dream is actually about becoming a more empowered version of herself.

That's the way I'd love for you to look at the outrageous dream you thought of a minute ago. Take another moment to go within and imagine who you will be when you are living that dream.

As you do, I think you'll begin to see how showing up in a bigger way actually serves the world.

It's not a selfish thing. So many of the wonderful innovations we enjoy today came from people who dared to dream big (despite the odds) and who showed up all the way.

When we give ourselves permission to dream bigger, we energetically give others permission to do the same, and everyone wins.

Carry your big dream inside you starting today, and give yourself plenty of chances to daydream about the *you* you're becoming.

DREAMS VS GOALS

Dreams are different than goals. Dreams are visions that express who we truly are. When we're completely in touch with the dreams and visions that express who we are at our core, it feels really, really good. It feels like *having*.

Goals are different because they bring with them a sense of pressure. They highlight the difference between where we are and where we want to be.

I think most of us look at our dreams as goals, and that gets in the way, because we're putting our focus on the space in between what we have and what we want. We're activating the lack in the equation, and that sets up a chain reaction that turns us in a direction facing away from our dream.

So many times we *force* ourselves to do the things we think we need to do in order to achieve a goal. (And even then we still don't always end up achieving it!)

So let's take a moment to sit with *your* big dream and see it not as something you have to think about, figure out, and do. Instead, let's think of it as a way you get to *be*. Think of yourself as a flower that just needs to bloom a little bit more.

Or think of yourself as a whole rosebush. Maybe right now you've got one or two blooms showing, but you've got the potential for so many more.

Blooming isn't a *goal* that a rosebush has. For a rosebush, blooming is just a matter of being in the right environment and soaking in the right things. And then what's meant to be just naturally happens.

In the right environment, with the right kind of support and nourishment, you (like the rosebush) just naturally express more and more of who you are.

No matter how long you've been disconnected from your dreams, I hope you are beginning to feel more and more that they are not only possible, but actually meant to be.

THE GUARDIAN OF YOUR DREAM

Bring your big dream to mind again, and resist the temptation to swap it out for another idea.

Tune in to your own energy field, and feel your house of self-love around you. Take a deep breath, let it out slowly, and as you do, drop energetic roots down into the Earth. Draw love from the Earth up your roots, and feel that love shimmer inside your house of self-love, strengthening and stabilizing it.

Gently focus your attention on your heart and say, "I love you."

As you continue to focus on the beauty of your own heart, connect to the energy of your Big Dream, and feel it living there in your heart.

Continue to feel your house of self-love around you and the love of the Earth nourishing you. Now, within this sacred space, ask that the Guardian of your dream come forth.

See or feel or sense this Guardian with you now, and recognize its power. Ask to receive its wisdom concerning your dream.

Open yourself now to fully receive the guidance, help, and support of this Guardian.

Let the beauty of the energy you feel fill your house of self-love now, and set an intention to stay centered within your house.

Feel the light from the Guardian of your dream shining forth from your heart and filling the room you're in now.

Radiate that beautiful light everywhere you go from now on!

GROUNDING YOUR DREAMS

We all have a tendency to live too much in our heads, and the more we do this, the more we may begin to think of our dreams as just fantasies.

So now let's embody the energy of our dreams, and ground them into every part of our being.

I believe it's a good practice to get into the habit of dropping energetic roots into the Earth all day long. Every time you do, take the opportunity to connect in your heart with all the wonderful things that you would like to do and be and have.

Hold your right hand to your heart and connect to a bigger, more fully expressed version of yourself, your "dreams-fulfilled self."

Connect to that version of yourself in your heart, activate its energy within you, and then spread that energy out into every part of your body. Feel the energy of your dreams fulfilled spread out all around you, and now ground it down into the Earth.

Just as nourishment flows up roots to support a Tree, feel the Earth's love flowing up through your roots and supporting you and your dreams.

Partner with the consciousness of the Earth to bring your dreams into physical reality. See yourself again as a beautiful rose or flowering bush, feeling the physical energy of the Earth supporting you in blooming forth in all kinds of ways—ways you may not even be able to imagine today.

I hope your dreams are waking up and feeling more and more alive within you as we move through this chapter together. I'm sending you love as you partner with the love of the Earth, shining the light of your dreams far and wide!

STRETCHING YOUR "DREAMING MUSCLES"

The more we connect to our dreams, the better we feel in our body, mind, and spirit. Now let's expand our idea of what's possible for us. We'll do this without getting attached to any particular outcome (because that's actually counterproductive).

Instead, we'll stretch our "dreaming muscles," with the intent of opening ourselves to all the wonder in the world that's just waiting for us to experience it.

We'll connect to the possibilities in our hearts, and we'll feel good just thinking about all the things we'd love to experience, *without* thinking about having to make them happen.

In this way, we'll expand our inner landscapes and allow ourselves to fully experience and express all the beauty that's in our hearts.

Bring to mind one of your heart's desires. Feel its energy already living in your heart, and let this energy make you smile.

Now allow this dream to expand to twice its size. Imagine a version of your dream that's twice as big and twice as wonderful.

For example, I love the Disneyland resort in Southern California. I'm so happy when I'm there—it really is a magical place for me. So let's say my original dream is to be on a wonderful trip to Disneyland. I can expand that dream and imagine that I've got trips planned to visit all the Disney parks, including those in other countries.

This may feel like being greedy. If so, you might want to take a deep breath and ground yourself before you go on.

Know that the purpose of our exercise is not to be greedy, but instead to expand our ability to experience more goodness—to expand our mindsets to fulfill the entire divine blueprint we carry within.

Living out the dreams of our hearts creates an energy of blessing that spreads out all around us.

Do this yourself with your own example now. How does it feel?

If you're feeling brave, connect to the love in your heart for your biggest dream and make it even bigger, not with a feeling of forcing, but just to expand your idea of what is possible for you, to expand beyond your own self-imposed boundaries.

When I expand on my Disneyland dream and give myself a chance to experience the magic at other parks, I am allowing more life energy to flow through me. It doesn't feel greedy—it feels expansive.

As you go through the days and weeks to come, identify the dreams of your heart for every area of your life. Do it in a balanced way, getting in touch with your dreams for your body, your relationships, your family, your home, and your work.

Let your love for your dreams fuel you. Be present, be open, and expand the boundaries of what's possible for you as you become one with your dreams.

CHAPTER 28

MOVING FORWARD
TOGETHER

I hope you're feeling a new sense of wonder as you identify more and more with the expanded self you are meant to be.

Imagine your future self as you read this list:

She lives within her house of self-love.

She is open to new possibilities.

She gives herself permission.

She trusts herself.

She reinvents herself whenever she chooses.

She is open to receive.

She owns her true voice.

She makes peace with wherever she is.

She continually upgrades her self-talk.

She releases the past.

She is comfortable being herself.

She is free of worrying about what other people think.

She reclaims her energy through forgiveness.

She tells herself new stories.

She has reclaimed her spark.

She focuses on what she Wants.

She claims and expresses her boundaries.

She is a caretaker of consciousness.

She supports herself with love.

She expects the best.

She dreams bigger.

She is part of a collective of love.

How did it feel to imagine yourself embodying and expressing these life-expanding qualities?

Now read through the list in the first-person, and take note of how you feel. Remember, these are not affirmations. This list is actually a tool you can use to determine exactly where you are out of balance.

Just notice which statements don't seem true as you read through the list (they will probably stand out to you in some way). Then go back to the corresponding chapters and use the journeys and exercises to bring yourself into alignment.

I live within my house of self-love.

I am open to new possibilities.

I give myself permission.

I trust myself.

I reinvent myself whenever I choose.

I am open to receive.

I own my true voice.

I make peace with wherever I am.

I continually upgrade my self-talk.

I release the past.

I am comfortable being myself.

I am free of worrying about what other people think.

I reclaim my energy through forgiveness.

I tell myself new stories.

I have reclaimed my spark.

I focus on what I Want.

I claim and express my boundaries.

I am a caretaker of consciousness.

I support myself with love.

I expect the best.

I dream bigger.

I am part of a collective of love.

You'll find this list in the Appendix for easy access. Read through it as a daily ritual, or use it prescriptively.

When you're feeling out of balance, you can flip to the pertinent chapter and easily find an exercise or journey that will shift you into a better state and connect you to the Guardians who will support you and help you evolve into your expanded self.

WE ARE GATEWAY GUARDIANS

I've got a final personal story for you, and it's a big one. I think the best way to tell it is to share with you an email I sent to the people on my Guardian Gateway email list last year.

I haven't been able to get in touch with you or post a new podcast episode recently because my dad has been having some health problems that have kept us in and out of the emergency room and doctors' offices.

He's feeling better right now, and I want to share something with you that happened during one of our ER visits. It was close to midnight, and even though I'd been supported by my Guardians, I was feeling depleted as I trudged through the empty hospital hallways on the way to the pharmacy.

Then I thought of all of you—a community of thousands, made up of all the people who have taken part in our telesummits throughout the years—and I felt enveloped in a huge wave of love and support.

It uplifted me so much! And I want to say two things about it:

(1) Thank you!

If you have ever felt appreciation or love for me and the work I do, I want to thank you for contributing to the energetic space that I tapped into that night at the ER.

(2) That energetic space remains there for all of us to tap into—it is filled with my love, your love, and the love of the Guardians, and you can access it at any time.

Thank you for helping to create the sacred space we continue to share!

After I sent this email, I received many responses from people who told me that they, too, felt the presence of this energetic space. This is *our* Guardian Gateway—a place of connection that connects you and me and everyone who shares this path. We can fill this sacred space with love and support when we are feeling balanced and centered, and draw love from it when we need support.

Go deep within your own heart and connect to the presence of your Greater Self there. Go deeper and deeper, until you become aware of the presence of a golden spark-like light.

As you focus on this spark of light, you see that it is the most special Gateway—the energetic meeting place where you and I and the Guardians and everyone who joins us in this sacred group connect.

Each of us came into this life already knowing and loving each other, ready to support one another in our mission to partner with the Guardians and bring forth every bit of the beauty and power within us.

You feel the power of the golden light increasing as you send it love, and you feel rays of this light spreading out in all directions, each ray connecting to a fellow traveler on this path.

Know that as you carry this light within your heart, you become a Guardian yourself—a Guardian of this and every other Gateway you tend through your attention and your love.

THANK YOU

As we come to the end of this book, I want to thank you from my heart for stepping forward to partner with the Guardians.

The world needs you to create a life that is the perfect expression of your beauty and your truth.

Ask the Guardian Beings at your side to help you know yourself, love yourself, and express yourself. Connect with them every day, asking for their help and support in everything you do, large and small.

In so doing, you'll bring more and more of your unique, beautiful energy into the world, blessing us all with the powerful energy of love that is at your core.

No matter how long you've struggled to create a life that matches your inner visions, don't give up. Now is the time our visions can come true, because now we are *together*.

Don't forget to go to KimWilborn.com/Bonus to get your free Guardian Gateway Expansion Bonus. This bonus includes special telesummit call recordings to help you create relationships with each Guardian plus an extra skill, Create a Personal Mission Statement, which will give you additional support as you journey through the book.

APPENDIX

Full-Length Guided Journey Preparation

If you find you want more help going deeply within, you can use the following guided journey as a preamble to the journeys you take in this book. (You should always be in a safe space with your full attention available—not driving—when you engage in a guided journey or exercise.)

Take a deep breath and let it out slowly as you prepare to fully enter into the sacred space we are creating together. With each breath, feel yourself relaxing more and more.

Allow yourself to feel a beautiful beam of Source energy entering through the top of your head. Let this energy flow down into your body, into every part of your being. Feel it filling your entire body, flowing through your feet, and beaming down into the center of the Earth.

At the center of the Earth, feel the presence of a huge glowing crystal filled with positive energy and love for you. See the beam of Source energy flow down into the crystal, harmonize with the energy there, and beam straight back up into you.

Feel this beautiful energy flow up through the soles of your feet, into your knees, up into your hips, your chest, your arms, your throat, and your head. Feel it filling your heart and spreading out all around you—and now feel it spread out to encompass the whole world. See the whole planet held in a space of safety.

Within this space of love and safety, feel yourself become centered.

Feel yourself become grounded.

Feel yourself become balanced.

And feel yourself become whole.

Now come back to your own heart, and from that heart space, open to connect with high-vibration Guardian Beings in all their many forms. Feel the beautiful, pure life force within you.

Feel the loving life force of the Earth supporting you, and feel the wisdom and love in the Guardian Energies all around you.

Feel yourself a vital part of this whole, and take your place in the creative tapestry of life that we are all weaving . . . together.

You may want to take your time returning after each journey and exercise:

Now come back to your normal waking state and send your energetic roots deeply down into the loving Earth.

Feel yourself fully in your body, and wiggle your fingers and toes for a few moments. Look around at the room or space you are in, and feel every part of your body full of the energy of life and love.

After each journey is complete, take a few moments to come fully back into your body. Always remember to say thank you (even if I don't remind you)! Saying thank you will remind you that you're not engaged in mental exercises—instead, you are connecting with real living, loving beings.

EXPANSION SKILLS CHECK-IN

Whenever you feel out of balance, read through the following list and notice which statements don't seem true (they will probably stand out to you in some way).

Then go back to the chapters with the corresponding skills you need to work on. (Each line corresponds with a skill from Chapters 6 through 28, in order.) Use the journeys and exercises to bring yourself back into alignment.

I live within my house of self-love.

I am open to new possibilities.

I give myself permission.

I trust myself.

I reinvent myself whenever I choose.

I am open to receive.

I own my true voice.

I make peace with wherever I am.

I continually upgrade my self-talk.

I release the past.

I am comfortable being myself.

I am free of worrying about what other people think.

I reclaim my energy through forgiveness.

I tell myself new stories.

I have reclaimed my spark.

I focus on what I Want.

I claim and express my boundaries.

I am a caretaker of consciousness.

I support myself with love.

I expect the best.

I dream bigger.

I am part of a collective of love.

BIBLIOGRAPHY

Bloom, William. *Working with Angels, Fairies, and Nature Spirits*. London, UK: Hachette Digital, 1998.

Doré, Carole. *Visualization—The Power of Your Heart Audio Program*. Newport Beach, CA: PowerVision Publishing, 1986.

Hicks, Esther, and Jerry Hicks. *Ask and It Is Given: Learning to Manifest Your Desires*. Carlsbad, CA: Hay House, Inc., 2004.

Ponder, Catherine. *Open Your Mind to Receive*. Camarillo, CA: DeVorss & Co., 2008.

Spangler, David. *Subtle Worlds: An Explorer's Field Notes*. Everett, WA: Lorian Press, 2010.

ACKNOWLEDGMENTS

In addition to my ongoing gratitude to the Guardians—and all who love them—I'd love to say a heartfelt thank you to so many special people in my life.

A big thank-you goes to Reid Tracy, my editor Nicolette Salamanca Young, and everyone at Hay House—I am thrilled to be part of the Hay House family!

All my telesummit speakers and listeners, and everyone in the Guardian Gateway community. I appreciate you so much!

A special thanks goes to Vicki Ridgeway Barton and Julie Nantel for being such wonderfully engaged participants in my *Daily Gateway* program, on which part of this book is based. Knowing you were there eagerly awaiting the daily messages made it *so* much easier to write them, and you both have a very special place in my heart!

My good friend and mastermind partner, Dr. Monique Hunt, for hours upon hours of work, food, and fun.

My "aunties" in spirit: Corolla Accurso, Rose Metowski, and Emily Cohen, for decades of love and support.

My forever friend, Glennie Noste: everyone should be lucky enough to have someone like you in their life!

My son, Jimmy, for always lending a helping hand (and lots of technical advice).

My daughter, Jenny, for being my best friend and partner in crime.

My mom and dad for being a rock-solid foundation and source of love and support. I know we've been the "Three Musketeers" in many lifetimes, and I'm so lucky to have had you with me in this one!

ABOUT THE AUTHOR

Kim Wilborn is a telesummit creator and host who also offers online learning programs that focus on connecting to spiritual Guardian energies. She specializes in sharing practical ways to develop relationships with spiritual Guardians and Allies, and teaches groundbreaking, transformational skills to help people fulfill their soul purpose. Prior to creating telesummits, she had an intuitive coaching and hypnotherapy practice. Her many years of work with clients gave her deep insight into the things that hold us back from fulfilling our soul purpose. Now, her driving mission in life is to help people gain the skills they need to experience the fulfillment that comes from showing up fully in life as who they are meant to be. *Website:* www.KimWilborn.com

We hope you enjoyed this Hay House book. If you'd like to receive our online catalog featuring additional information on Hay House books and products, or if you'd like to find out more about the Hay Foundation, please contact:

Hay House, Inc., P.O. Box 5100, Carlsbad, CA 92018-5100
(760) 431-7695 or (800) 654-5126
(760) 431-6948 (fax) or (800) 650-5115 (fax)
www.hayhouse.com® • www.hayfoundation.org

Published in Australia by: Hay House Australia Pty. Ltd.,
18/36 Ralph St., Alexandria NSW 2015
Phone: 612-9669-4299 • *Fax:* 612-9669-4144
www.hayhouse.com.au

Published in the United Kingdom by: Hay House UK, Ltd.,
The Sixth Floor, Watson House, 54 Baker Street, London W1U 7BU
Phone: +44 (0)20 3927 7290 • *Fax:* +44 (0)20 3927 7291
www.hayhouse.co.uk

Published in India by: Hay House Publishers India,
Muskaan Complex, Plot No. 3, B-2, Vasant Kunj, New Delhi 110 070
Phone: 91-11-4176-1620 • *Fax:* 91-11-4176-1630
www.hayhouse.co.in

Access New Knowledge.
Anytime. Anywhere.

Learn and evolve at your own pace
with the world's leading experts.

www.hayhouseU.com

Free e-newsletters from Hay House, the Ultimate Resource for Inspiration

Be the first to know about Hay House's free downloads, special offers, giveaways, contests, and more!

 Get exclusive excerpts from our latest releases and videos from *Hay House Present Moments.*

 Our *Digital Products Newsletter* is the perfect way to stay up-to-date on our latest discounted eBooks, featured mobile apps, and Live Online and On Demand events.

 Learn with real benefits! *HayHouseU.com* is your source for the most innovative online courses from the world's leading personal growth experts. Be the first to know about new online courses and to receive exclusive discounts.

 Enjoy uplifting personal stories, how-to articles, and healing advice, along with videos and empowering quotes, within *Heal Your Life.*

Sign Up Now!

Get inspired, educate yourself, get a complimentary gift, and share the wisdom!

Visit www.hayhouse.com/newsletters to sign up today!

Listen. Learn. Transform.

Find fulfillment with unlimited Hay House audios!

Connect with your soul, step into your purpose, and embrace joy with world-renowned authors and teachers—all in the palm of your hand. With the *Hay House Unlimited* Audio app, you can learn and grow in a way that fits your lifestyle . . . and your daily schedule.

With your membership, you can:

- Expand your consciousness, reclaim your purpose, deepen your connection with the Divine, and learn to love and trust yourself fully.

- Explore thousands of audiobooks, meditations, immersive learning programs, podcasts, and more.

- Access exclusive audios you won't find anywhere else.

- Experience completely unlimited listening. No credits. No limits. No kidding.

Try for FREE!

Visit **hayhouse.com/audioapp** to start your free trial and get one step closer to living your best life.

Listen. Learn. Transform.

Find fulfillment with
unlimited Hay House audios

Connect with your soul, step into your purpose, and embrace joy with world-renowned authors and teachers—all in the palm of your hand. With the Hay House Unlimited Audio app, you can learn and grow in a way that fits your lifestyle ... and your daily schedule.

With your membership, you can:

- Expand your consciousness, reclaim your purpose, deepen your connection with the Divine, and learn to love and trust yourself fully

- Explore thousands of audiobooks, meditations, immersive learning programs, podcasts, and more

- Access exclusive audios you won't find anywhere else.

- Experience completely unlimited listening. No credits. No limits. No kidding.

Try for FREE!